Fashion Design

Published by Laurence King Publishing
361–373 City Road
London EC1V 1LR
United Kingdom

Tel: +44 20 7841 6900
Email: enquiries@laurenceking.com
www.laurenceking.com

A catalogue record for this book is available from the British Library

ISBN: 978-1-78627-576-9

Front cover image Mark Hann/RooM/Getty Images.
Back cover image by Constance Blackaller.

Design: TwoSheds
Picture Research: Giulia Hetherington
Printed in China

Laurence King Publishing is committed to ethical and sustainable production. We are proud participants in The Book Chain Project®.
bookchainproject.com

Fashion Design

A Guide to the Industry and the Creative Process   Denis Antoine

Laurence King Publishing

Contents

Introduction

Fashion design is often a misunderstood discipline. The public perception of this field commonly focuses on extolling the instinctive creative abilities of genius designers, and intentionally minimizes the discussion of the diligent process that takes place behind the scenes. This book was developed specifically to guide the reader though this exciting, yet relatively obscure, subject.

Fashion designers at all levels of the industry face the challenging task of blending business and art toward the creation of relevant, commercially viable, and creatively exciting products every season. Additionally, all participants in the fashion industry, be they visual merchandisers, photographers, stylists, pattern-makers or buyers, benefit greatly from complete understanding of the creative process employed by designers. Fashion brands, after all, differentiate themselves primarily by *how* and *why* they create product, and by the artistic vision they offer, not simply by the items produced. To fully comprehend how fashion products are generated demands a thorough awareness of a multitude of sectors, which are best grouped in three main categories: context, concept, and presentation.

Context refers to the essential knowledge of the core historical facts and business structures employed in the fashion industry. Designers must possess a fluent familiarity with these points in order for their work to fit effectively within the current fashion marketplace. Key points of fashion history and business, introduction of current issues affecting the industry, as well as essential knowledge of brand development, consumer research, and trends are therefore addressed in Chapters 1 and 2, to provide a foundation from which to extend into creative endeavors.

Chapters 3, 4, and 5 focus on *concept* development, and discuss the processes required to generate new products for the fashion industry. From defining inspiration, to gathering research and applying it to original textile and design development, this section identifies the multitude of possible tools and techniques available when approaching the creative process. While the techniques discussed are relevant to many designers' methodologies, they should be regarded as a springboard of creative strategies and used by the reader as a jumping-off point for more advanced individual exploration and experimentation.

Once design development has been completed, and a new line is taking shape, fashion designers put into effect a variety of *presentation* tools, to convey the value of the new product. The type of presentation approach required differs greatly depending on the intended audience for the work. As such, some presentation methods, such as flats, are technically focused, while fashion illustrations are grounded in editorial narrative. The various presentation techniques used by fashion designers are, therefore, the subject of Chapter 6. Just as demonstrating fluency in a multitude of approaches to visual presentation is vital for young designers aiming to enter the industry, so is the ability to compile their work in a professional portfolio, addressing both physical and digital formats, and to deliver a compelling presentation verbally at a recruitment interview. For this reason, the final chapter provides guidance related to portfolio design, as well as résumé and interview tips.

While the fashion industry is the subject of constant evolution and challenge (both stylistically and structurally), the role of the fashion designer will remain pivotal to the success of this industry. Fashion designers are history buffs, strategic problem-solvers, business executives, painters, sculptors, technologists, and expert communicators all rolled into one. This book endeavors to elucidate this exciting creative role for all those interested in joining the fashion industry.

Opposite: Collage by Ashley Kang.

1. The history and business of fashion

Learning objectives

- Appreciate the various ways in which fashion can be understood: as a cultural product, a designed object, and as an industry

- Learn the key terminology pertaining to the study of fashion

- Understand the main historical developments that have affected the evolution of fashion

- Gain familiarity with key fashion designers from the 1800s to today

- Comprehend the structure of the fashion marketplace

- Be aware of the current issues impacting the fashion industry and its design practices

Understanding Fashion

Fashion is a hybrid discipline. It sits at the intersection of art, craft, and industry as both a creative practice and big business. To gain success and relevance, a designer's work must combine artistry with function, and be commercially viable. Before delving into the research, creative development, and presentation undertaken by designers and merchandisers in this industry, let's look at what fashion actually is.

Fashion is a cultural product

Just as music and art express esthetic preferences, fashion conveys the chosen dress codes of a particular group. **Taste** represents the embodiment of cultural preferences, often referred to as the culture's **Zeitgeist**. As culture changes, so does taste, and fashion follows along.

Fashion, by its very definition, is temporary. Most theorists agree that fashion does not simply refer to the clothing we wear; it also expresses a cultural language. Fashion is intrinsically bound by culture, as people who share cultural identity most likely share similar taste. For instance, young people in metropolitan cities such as Seoul and New York often share more similar style preferences with each other than with their local rural counterparts. These boundaries, which used to be very strict, are constantly being redrawn by social media and other forms of digital communication.

Opposite: Catwalk shows are just one of the many facets of the fashion industry.

Fashion terminology definitions

Dress: *The collective term describing all items and practices used by a population to protect and adorn the human body. As such, jewelry, clothing, makeup, footwear, and many more are all "items of dress."*

Clothing/Apparel: *Items of dress serving the primary purpose of covering the body, achieving both functional protection from the elements and moral propriety.*

Costume: *A style of dress that communicates belonging to a specific cultural group, social class, or national identity. Costume may also refer to a historical style, such as the Spanish farthingale, popular in the 16th century, and to national dress styles, such as Bavarian lederhosen: both are forms of costume while not qualifying as contemporary fashion. Costume tends not to change over time.*

Fashion: *A style that, at its peak, gains temporary popularity and widespread use, only to be replaced by a different style shortly afterward. This may refer to modes of dress, music, food, or any other consumer product. The word "fashion" is commonly used as synonym for the most popular style of dress.*

Designer fashion showcased in a Moscow boutique.

Fashion is a designed object

Fashion is actively generated by designers. To enter this industry is to take on the challenge of pushing its esthetic language further through creative exploration and artistic process. As is evident from the definitions presented above, many of these concepts overlap, and there are several gray areas between each of these terms. However, it is important to pay close attention to the intended function of each form of dress in order to better hone the purpose of one's design practice and artistic choices. A large part of successfully designing fashion rests in the designer's ability to critically evaluate how their creative production connects with its cultural and esthetic context. In this context a fashion designer's job is not only to design clothing or **apparel**, but to create constantly new styles that gain widespread acceptance and popularity. Failing to understand clearly how one's work relates to the taste preferences of an ever-changing society is very risky, and may cause designers to spend vast amounts of time, energy, and financial resources in the development of irrelevant and unsuccessful products. After all, fashion remains an economic pursuit. Only design innovations that present meaningful solutions to the needs, both functional and esthetic, of a real audience become financial successes.

Fashion is an industry

In addition to being a social phenomenon and the product of the creative talents of designers, fashion is a thriving industry. It is a powerful contributor to the global economy, operating through a worldwide **supply chain** that employs tens of millions of people, from cotton pickers in Uzbekistan to yarn spinners in Peru and **retailers** in Japan. Joining this discipline as a designer, merchandiser, or **product developer** requires a thorough understanding of both the phenomenal potential of the existing system, as well as its deep structural failings, some of which will be addressed in more detail later in this chapter (see page 26). While methods of communication have been revolutionized by the introduction of the Internet in the

1990s, the way we make garments has not changed substantially since the Industrial Revolution in the late 18th century. Designers and all other creative thinkers wanting to make a meaningful contribution to the fashion industry, and to see it thrive in the future, must therefore apply their creativity and artistry not just to develop beautiful products, but also to provide innovative, real, and sustainable solutions to how fashion is designed, made, distributed, and sold.

Above: A designer studio in Seoul where new apparel is developed.
Below: One of the many steps in the fashion industry, a textile production facility.

Fashion History Overview

A designer's ability to make informed creative decisions is strengthened by an awareness of the historical context of fashion. For this reason, it is essential to gain a basic understanding of the history behind the fashion industry and the stylistic choices we see around us today. The overview below presents a brief outline of key themes, but for a more thorough appreciation of the historical context of fashion, consult the material listed in Useful Resources (see page 214).

While the industry has globalized in terms of production and manufacturing, the esthetics developed in Europe, North America, and Japan still direct the visual language of global fashion. For this reason the following synopsis focuses predominantly on these regions.

One concept commonly associated with fashion is that of luxury. While "fashion" indicates a temporary style preference, "luxury" is focused on value. Well before the recognizable appearance of fashion in Europe, cultures around the world had developed a clear understanding of luxury. Products and materials were classified according to their rarity and difficulty of access. The scarcer the resource, the more expensive it became, and the more luxurious it was perceived to be. Silk traded from China, rare dyes, gold, and precious stones were prevalent throughout the ancient world as obvious symbols of status. In many ways the symbolic codes of luxury have not evolved substantially since then.

The beginning of European fashion

The majority of fashion historians agree that the cultural phenomenon of fashion can be visibly recognized for the first time in Europe around the 13th century. Prior to this time, styles changed very slowly. A pivotal shift fueled by the rapid growth of production and trade occurred in the later **Middle Ages**. Technological innovations, such as the spinning wheel and the mechanized weaving loom (also known as a dobby loom), made it possible to produce fabric much faster than ever before, and new materials and

Portraits showed new styles in the early days of fashion. Loyset Liedet, *The Wedding of Renaud de Montauban*, c.1462–70.

techniques were brought from the Middle East as a result of the Crusades. The evolution of the European aristocratic courts, and the improvement of both verbal and visual communication, provided both the stage for and the means of raising awareness of new styles. Now, dominant **silhouettes** and popular garments enjoyed only brief acceptance, and were replaced much more rapidly. Competition between the various courts around the Continent provided the motivation to pursue new and intriguing garments, accessories, and forms of dress.

Antonio del Pollaiuolo, *Portrait of a Young Lady*, c.1465.

Aristocratic Rococo style on display. François Boucher, *Madame de Pompadour*, 1756.

This Charles Dana Gibson illustration showcases the simpler dress styles popularized by the Industrial Revolution. *The Sweetest Story Ever Told*, c.1910.

The age of imperialism

Starting in the late 1400s with the Spanish and Portuguese expansion of sea trade across the Atlantic, colonization of the Americas, and the establishment of maritime routes to India, European powers focused on garnering vast economic resources by conquering territories around the world. The courts of Spain, England, and later France became the arena for spectacularly lavish displays of wealth. Extravagance, always synonymous with power and social rank, was made even more visible through the use of exotic materials and labor-intensive techniques. Sheer cotton muslins, handmade lace, pearls, and precious stones embodied their wearers' economic and political standing. The establishment of the French court of Louis XIV at Versailles (1682) is considered by many to be the start of the virtual monopoly on new fashions held by France until the 20th century.

The Industrial Revolution

The introduction of new technology in the late 18th century contributed to the swift expansion of mass-production. Industrial equipment, including the cotton gin, high-yield carding machines, the power loom, and the sewing machine revolutionized apparel production. By the mid-1800s, mass-manufacturing of commercial goods was well established, and for the first time in history, **ready-to-wear** apparel was easily accessible for the populations of Europe and North America. Fashion was no longer the exclusive prerogative of the aristocracy. Mass-retailers at newly established department stores, such as Macy's and Lord & Taylor, sold simplified copies of the fashionable styles coming from France. Much of the technology and many of the production processes developed during that period are still used today.

Audrey Hepburn embodying the style of the modern woman, 1950s.

The modern age

Industrialization led to the growth of urban populations and marked the beginnings of the modern age. Luxury pursuits were no longer exclusively centered on extravagant goods, but started to include a new focus on leisure. The ability to vacation and take part in sports such as tennis and golf became visible expressions of economic power and social standing. Women became increasingly involved in the workforce and politics. Urban populations required functional, user-friendly fashions, and the impractical dressing of the past was replaced with simple, easy-to-wear, and inherently democratic styles. The focus on function was at the core of the first phase of the modern age, from the late 19th century to the 1960s. Cultural

fragmentation, including the youthquake, women's liberation, and civil-rights movements, opened the Pandora's box of pluralism – the idea that Western society must be inclusive of multiple opinions and viewpoints, and that a society held to a single unified ideology is untenable. This period marked the beginning and established the philosophical tenets of postmodernity, considered by many as a second phase of the modern era. While modernism is most commonly defined by functional design and simplified esthetics, **postmodernism** takes the mass-production, distribution, and communication made possible by the modern age and forges new applications from them, focused on expressiveness and entertainment.

Key Designers

Charles Frederick Worth (British, 1825–95)

A British cloth merchant, Worth became the first designer of fashion in the late 1800s. He was the first to showcase seasonal collections of garments to his elite customers, and to label garments made by his house with tags bearing his own name. Prior to Worth, members of the elite would purchase fabrics and have their tailors or seamstresses make outfits based on the styles they had seen at court. Worth introduced the notion that the designer, not the customer, should lead the way in introducing new fashionable styles. He single-handedly codified French *haute couture* and established the Chambre Syndicale de la Haute Couture (Syndicated Chamber of Haute Couture), the trade organization that continues to control this exclusive **market level**.

Paul Poiret (French, 1879–1944)

At the beginning of the 20th century, Poiret envisioned fashion stepping away from the outdated esthetic codes of court dressing. His work was inspired by Orientalism, the Ballets Russes, and fantasy. As the first designer to present women's styles that did not require corseting, Poiret paved the way for the modernization of fashion throughout the rest of the century.

Mariano Fortuny (Spanish, 1871–1949)

Working from Venice rather than Paris, Fortuny developed an esthetic approach that made truly radical departures from traditional dressmaking. His Delphos dress, constructed of finely pleated silk, was reminiscent of ancient Greek costume, and was the first stretch garment in Western history. It allowed its wearer a freedom of movement unknown in Europe since the Middle Ages.

Coco Chanel (French, 1883–1971)

Chanel recognized that society was changing around her, and created styles that embraced these changes. Her use of **jersey** fabrics, soft tweeds, and loose cuts made her work both functionally and esthetically relevant to the 1920s. Her boyish silhouettes and pared-down **color palette** reflected the changing role of women after World War I.

Madeleine Vionnet (French, 1876–1975)

Vionnet invented the **bias** cut, which involved cutting diagonally. This gave woven fabrics, such as crepes and satins, semi-stretch properties, and allowed Vionnet to create garments that flowed with natural elegance, and permitted movement and comfort for their wearers.

Elsa Schiaparelli (Italian, 1890–1973)

Schiaparelli's inventive style was highly influential in the late 1930s, and still inspires brands such as Comme des Garçons, Maison Martin Margiela, and Viktor & Rolf. She fostered artistic collaborations with her Surrealist friends Salvador Dalí and Jean Cocteau, and effectively originated the notion of **conceptual design** in the field of fashion.

Christian Dior (French, 1905–57)

Dior's silhouettes, introduced in 1947 and known as the "New Look," redefined femininity. During the 1930s and World War II women worked in traditionally masculine roles in factories, construction, and the army. With inventive use of new materials such as nylon, and taking inspiration from the hourglass silhouettes of the 19th century, Dior envisioned a romantic, hyper-feminine fashion that resonated with women in the late 1940s and early 1950s.

Christian Dior, "New Look," 1947.

Cristóbal Balenciaga (Spanish, 1895–1972)

Balenciaga was considered by his contemporaries, and by most designers since, as a master's master. His approach to cut and volume was more akin to sculpture than traditional dressmaking. He collaborated with textile mills to create new materials that would support his groundbreaking silhouettes without hindering movement and function.

Yves Saint Laurent (French, 1936–2008)

The first creator to embrace the esthetic principles of postmodern design, Yves Saint Laurent took inspiration from diverse cultures and social groups not traditionally considered sources of fashionable dress. His tuxedo for women, known in French as *Le Smoking*, blurred gender boundaries and showcased a newly empowered vision of femininity.

Halston (American, 1932–90)

The dominant American fashion designer of the 1970s, Halston (always known just by his surname) presented a signature style that blended simplicity and elegance. He made extensive use of bias cutting to create statuesque and luxurious silhouettes. His shirtwaist dress and cashmere twinset established the esthetic language of minimalism in fashion.

Vivienne Westwood (British, born 1941)

Westwood brought punk to fashion. Heavily involved in the subcultural youth scene of 1970s London, she presented a vision of fashion that removed the traditional status-focus boundaries of style. Her work regularly references nihilism and anti-conformism, mixing high and low, couture and trash.

Issey Miyake (Japanese, born 1938)

The primary focus of Miyake rests in technological innovation. He collaborates with industrial engineers and fiber scientists to explore new ways to construct garments. He was the first to introduce ultrasuede in the 1970s, and is well known for his A-POC and Pleats Please lines.

Rei Kawakubo (Japanese, born 1942)

Kawakubo's brand, Comme des Garçons, bends all the rules of how fashion is traditionally designed and made. Her avant-garde work is conceived through abstract conceptual processes that generate unexpected, radical, and sometimes jarring outcomes. Kawakubo's way of working established the creative platform from which designers such as Martin Margiela and Helmut Lang evolved.

Yohji Yamamoto (Japanese, born 1943)

The traditional Japanese ideology of *wabi-sabi*, which embraces the beauty of imperfection, dominates the creative production of Yamamoto. His work intentionally appears rough, unfinished, or worn out.

John Galliano (British, born 1960)

Heavily influenced by Kawakubo's conceptualism and Westwood's subculture-focused design approach, Galliano developed a style that could best be described as "historical collage." His work embraces the expressiveness of postmodernism and presents a "more is more" vision of esthetics. He is known primarily for the extravagant work he produced while creative director at Christian Dior and Maison Martin Margiela.

Alexander McQueen (British, 1969–2010)

Revered by many as the most influential designer of the early 21st century, Alexander McQueen blended history, costume, art, and fashion, in the process redefining what the discipline could accomplish. His collections were displayed in ways more like performance art than runway presentations, and his style combined traditional luxury, romantic elegance, and assertive self-empowerment.

Charles Frederick Worth

Coco Chanel

Christian Dior

Paul Poiret

Madeleine Vionnet

Cristóbal Balenciaga

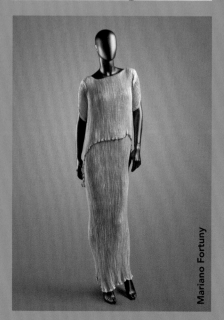

Mariano Fortuny

Elsa Schiaparelli

Yves Saint Laurent

Rei Kawakubo

Halston

Vivienne Westwood

Yohji Yamamoto

John Galliano

Issey Miyake

Alexander McQueen

The Fashion Marketplace

To be able to contribute effectively to design and **merchandising** in this challenging industry, it is essential to acquire an understanding of the existing structures upon which the fashion industry is formed. Businesses operate in a variety of areas, and have the ability to choose their preferred price bracket and define their ideal merchandising strategy. Understanding each of these possible directions provides a valuable core upon which further discussion of research and design process can be grounded.

Business categories

As an initial step in furthering a clear understanding of the fashion industry, let's look at the three primary types of company that drive this worldwide business: retailers, manufacturers, and contractors.

Retailers sell products to the user or consumer. A retail business may be an independent luxury boutique like Brown's in London, or a multibillion-dollar behemoth like TopShop. Retailers most often operate through multiple channels, including brick-and-mortar stores, as well as digital platforms such as e-tailing and mobile shopping.

Manufacturers create new products and sell them to retailers. Usually, fashion manufacturers launch new merchandise through runway shows or presentations at trade shows, such as Pitti Uomo (Florence, Italy) or the Magic Marketplace (Las Vegas, Nevada). These companies generate revenue primarily by selling their designs at **wholesale** prices to retailers. Some manufacturers may also operate a few branded "flagship stores" directly.

Contractors make the merchandise sold by retailers. These companies produce apparel, accessories, and other fashion products according to the design specifications provided

Above: Retailers often position themselves in concentrated settings, such as high streets or shopping malls, as here in Munich, Germany.
Right: Harrods in London is an iconic luxury department store.

by the manufacturers, and in the quantities requested by the retailers. Contractors are often specialized in an area of apparel production, such as cut-and-sew knits, print production, denim, or tailoring. With the exception of higher-priced production in Europe, Japan, South Korea, and North America, the vast majority of apparel contractors in recent decades have been located in countries such as Pakistan, Bangladesh, Vietnam, and China. These countries have lower minimum wages, which reduce the cost of production and allow retailers to sell at cheaper prices. The employment regulations in these nations are also much more conducive to the interests of large retailers.

Companies that operate in multiple areas simultaneously use a strategy called **vertical integration**. For example, Zara has established a very successful business model by controlling all its retail and product development, as well as gaining direct control of most of its production facilities and its material development. This enables the company to be extremely flexible and responsive to the needs of its customers, introducing new product offerings multiple times each week.

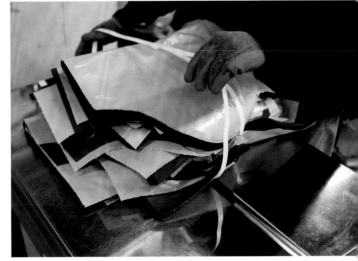

Top: Dries van Noten, a fashion manufacturer, showcases new collections to buyers and the press through runway presentations.
Above: Garment pieces cut and ready for production at a fashion-contractor factory.

Right: Guo Pei Haute Couture, Fall 2018.
Below: Valentino Haute Couture, Fall 2018.

Market levels

Another important distinction in the fashion marketplace is the **market level**, or pricing bracket, that manufacturers, retailers, and contractors may operate within.

Haute couture is a French phrase meaning literally "high sewing," though the term is often misused as a synonym for "high-end" fashion. The precise definition of *haute couture* is custom-designed and custom-made products created and produced exclusively for one client, often involving extensive use of hand **construction** methods. *Haute couture*, by its nature, cannot be produced in multiple samples in standard sizes. Chanel, Christian Dior, Armani Privé, Elie Saab, and Viktor & Rolf are brands operating at this level of the marketplace. In France, this level is regulated by the Chambre Syndicale de la Haute Couture, which determines which designers may officially show and sell their work as *haute couture*. The organization protects the integrity of this market level as an important part of French cultural heritage.

Ready-to-wear (RTW) is the name given to any garments produced in standard sizes and multiple quantities. The term does not reflect the pricing level of the garment. It could, in fact, be any of the following:

Designer market level is occupied by high-end, RTW lines that usually carry the name of the designer or house. Designers focused on *haute couture* utilize this level to make their brand attainable by a broader audience. Valentino RTW, Alexander McQueen, Gucci, and Prada are all examples of this market level.

Bridge level, often used as a brand **diffusion** opportunity, sits between designer pricing and brand-name broad distribution merchandise. Vivienne Westwood Red Label, Marc by Marc Jacobs, and Michael Kors sit in this category.

Better level products are designed and produced in more elevated fabrics and finishes than the average product available in the broad distribution marketplace. Brands such as J. Crew, Banana Republic, Esprit, French Connection, and COS are all good examples of this level.

Moderate level is broadly prevalent in **high street** or mall brands. Gap, H&M, Zara, and most of the well-known chain brands around the world operate within this space.

Budget (or mass-market) is the lowest pricing level and usually associated with discounters and off-price brands. This segment of the industry is represented by retailers such as Walmart, Old Navy, T.J./T.K. Maxx, and Primark.

Right: Vivienne Westwood MAN,
a bridge-level brand.
Below: Banana Republic, a better-level
retailer, in Singapore.

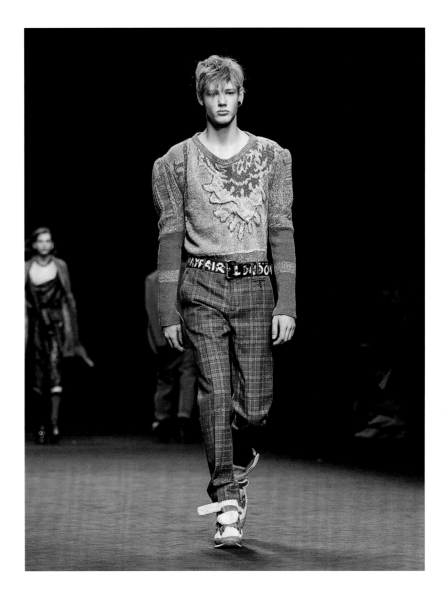

Merchandising strategies

Companies at all marketplace levels must adopt a clear strategic approach to design and creative presentation. Merchandising strategy is critical in establishing a strong brand direction and generating effective brand messaging. Designers and product developers may choose from three directions: innovation, interpretation, or imitation.

Design innovators do not follow trends; they create product in artistically focused processes. Their creative output flows from novel, unique, and sometimes extreme perspectives. While their vision may find a cult following, innovators are often at the higher end of the pricing spectrum and are generally smaller companies willing to take creative risks for the sake of their artistry. Comme des Garçons, Issey Miyake, Vivienne Westwood, and Alexander McQueen are strong examples of design innovators.

Left: Thom Browne, a design innovator presenting uncompromising designs on the runway.
Right: As a design interpreter, Etro showcases a careful blend of creativity and wearability.

Design interpreters are more restricted artistically than innovators. They often blend inventive processes with a strong awareness of what their competitors and retailers are doing. Awareness and implementation of retail trends in their work allows them to produce lines that appeal to a broader audience. Etro, Narciso Rodriguez, Alberta Ferretti, and Monique Lhuillier all represent this merchandising approach. By taking this direction, these companies are able to develop product that still feels creatively valuable, while also being easy for their customers to implement in their day-to-day lifestyles.

Zara is well known for developing a successful business focused on the design-imitator strategy.

Design imitators are companies that rely on taking their creative cues directly from other brands or from street style. Companies such as Zara and H&M have a very strong focus on profitability, and choose not to dedicate a lot of financial resources on fostering the artistic impulses of their designers. They instead focus on making effective, strategically informed selections of product styles from other runways or from **trend** reports by companies such as WGSN. This approach, combined with a very swift production and distribution strategy, makes it possible for these imitators to produce a vast number of different styles at inexpensive prices, in turn generating vast profits.

Contrary to much of the press narrative surrounding fashion, which focuses heavily on innovators and interpreters, it is the budget and moderate imitator brands that operate as some of the largest, most powerful companies in this industry. For example, according to 2017

financial reporting, Inditex, the parent company of Zara, generated sales of more than €25 billion, while Kering, one of the most influential luxury conglomerates, controlling brands such as Balenciaga, Alexander McQueen, Gucci, Bottega Veneta, and Saint Laurent, posted total revenues of only €15.5 billion. These figures also reflect the number of career opportunities available within those markets: total employment in the budget market greatly exceeds that at the luxury end of the industry.

Educational institutions training the future fashion workforce are adapting to these changes. While many institutions and programs focus on creativity and artistry, which is essential in the formation of strong designers, they have also added courses that foster an understanding of context, current industry challenges, and business awareness.

Current Issues in the Fashion Industry

When considered from a historical perspective, the fashion industry is surprisingly young. Mass-production of commercial goods, including fashion, only became a reality in the late 19th century. And just like any other fledgling human endeavor, the industry has displayed some serious growing pains, particularly in recent decades.

The impact of cost-driven supply-chain management

Many companies have become accustomed to selecting a supply chain of dealers and contractors exclusively on the basis of cost. This has led to many retailers supporting a variety of ethically unacceptable processes, such as sweatshops and child labor. This cost-driven decision-making strategy has had several negative impacts, which have become the subject of much soul-searching in the trade. These concerns have led to many companies developing frameworks for social responsibility, the idea being that companies should support the welfare of society at large and be held accountable for their actions.

Fair employment practices

The cost-driven model has directly supported the widespread growth of forced, underpaid, or abusive employment practices. This has come into the public eye very starkly through events such as the Rana Plaza disaster of 2013 in Bangladesh, when a building containing garment factories collapsed and killed 1,134 workers. Many companies are changing their sourcing practices to ensure that their product is manufactured exclusively in factories that abide by acceptable employment standards. The problem that remains to be overcome is that much production in Asia is subcontracted to a vast array of additional facilities, often without proper disclosure to the **manufacturer**.

The growth of the handmade movement and the resurgence of craft-driven companies that produce locally and transparently are likely outcomes of the increased awareness of ethical approaches to labor.

Environmental impact

Environmental-impact analyses of the fashion industry often place it as the second most polluting, preceded only by the fossil-fuel industry. This environmental toll is caused by both the production of the raw materials necessary for apparel production and the vast carbon footprint generated by the distribution networks enabling the operation of global supply chains. Furthermore, the very basis of the current profit model fueling this industry is rooted in waste. To make revenues soar, fashion businesses need to encourage consumers to buy new styles before their existing clothes become functionally unwearable. Planned obsolescence, the idea that garments that are not on trend or in season should be discarded and replaced with new styles, is fundamentally in opposition to the principles of environmental sustainability.

Growing public awareness of this issue means the industry is bound to change in the not-so-distant future, and designers, creative directors, and all engaged leaders in our field will have to adapt accordingly.

Opposite, above and below: Garment workers in developing economies play an essential part in the current global fashion supply chain (below in Dhaka, Bangladesh).

THE FASHION SUPPLY CHAIN,
FROM LINEAR TO CIRCULAR

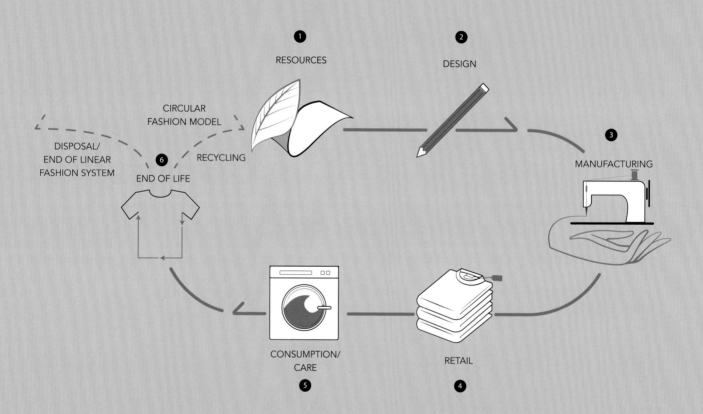

Redefining retail: a virtual changing room by Urban Research, Japan.

Operating in a fully sustainable manner requires very precise awareness of how each step of sourcing, production, and distribution impacts the environment. This encompasses organic fiber production, or using fabrics made of fully recycled and recyclable materials, embracing alternatives to toxic dyes, and making clear calculations of how producing and transporting apparel around the world requires vast amounts of fossil fuels.

While some fashion companies, such as H&M and Kering, have made attempts at implementing environmental sustainability in their design and production practices, such efforts are often very limited in scope. Instead of being genuine systemic solutions, many amount to little more than promotional opportunities.

Among the true leaders in this field, Patagonia stands visibly in a class of its own. This brand's entire model focuses on environmental awareness, which has led not only to its extensive use of recycled fibers, but also to its deeply ingrained belief in the value of durability. This principle is implemented in every aspect of the brand, even going as far as encouraging its consumers to mend and repair old product instead of discarding and replacing it.

Current challenges to traditional retail

The rise of digital media and online retailing have impacted traditional retail models in fundamental ways. The outdated notion of brick-and-mortar stores stocking up with new product only a few times a year does not meet public expectation of constant innovation. Consumers now comparison-shop and purchase anything they wish online or on their cell phones within minutes. They also have instant access to products coming from around the globe. Physical retail stores must redefine their role, as they are outpaced and outperformed by the new formats. Forward-thinking brick-and-mortar retailers understand the unique possibilities afforded by digital platforms, and are integrating these within their physical environment to offer experiences that are truly exciting and new.

The digital age has opened the doors to the possibility of mass-customization. Companies such as Converse and Nike have used online platforms to allow shoppers to customize their preferred styles, choosing colors, **trims**, and details, and having those selections made to order. In recent years, a wide variety of brands have started offering customized, made-to-measure services that are enhanced by the intuitive access provided by online and mobile formats.

Designer Profile: Christopher Raeburn

Christopher Raeburn is the creative director of RÆBURN. Since this profile was compiled, he was appointed global creative director at Timberland.

Tell us about what made you want to be a designer.

I grew up in the countryside in a small village in Kent, in England. My upbringing focused on the outdoors and inventing. From the age of 11, I joined the air cadets and learned to fly. I therefore developed a fascination for military clothing and original functional fabrics from an early age. The truth is, I'm still not convinced that I'm a normal fashion designer. My interest is in the process, utility, and functionality – researching something and making sure it's worthwhile at the end, something that's considered in different ways. I'd therefore like to think I'm as much of a product designer as a fashion designer.

How would you describe your brand?

Everything we do as a business is underpinned by what we call the 4 R's: REMADE, REDUCED, RECYCLED, and RÆBURN. REMADE is about deconstructing and

reconstructing original items – we've used items like life rafts, military blankets, hot-air balloons ... you name it. Every REMADE piece is a limited edition, proudly cut and reconstructed in our studio in east London. REDUCED is all about minimizing carbon footprint, using organic cottons and working with local manufacturing. RECYCLED is about reusing pre-existing materials and harnessing green technologies. For example, a lot of our outerwear is made from plastic water bottles that have been ground down into pellets, then shredded into fiber and rewoven into fabric.

Why did you choose your specific niche? What opportunities has it provided you?

The truth is the niche chose me. I'm always very open that I didn't set out to start a sustainable company at all. I started using recycled materials from the very beginning. When I was at university there was something very exciting about going out and finding original items, and then making them into something new. My fascination with military materials, utilitarian clothing, and essential functionality led organically to the REMADE IN ENGLAND philosophy. I also found out five years after starting the business that my grandma had got married in a dress made from parachute silk. This really fascinated me and is a really nice case of serendipity.

I started the brand almost ten years ago now, and ultimately it's allowed me to grow a business, have a fantastic team, and work with some of the best brands in the world.

How do your chosen customer and market influence your design approach?

We have been working hard on defining our target customer as part of marketing strategy through analysis, research, and brand positioning, and as a result have identified opportunities with four distinctive types of customer, all men or women in their thirties, who seek good design quality and a brand story. Provenance of each item is very important for our customer. Part of the reason we've started opening up the RÆBURN Lab at weekends is to actually meet our customers. It's been very rewarding to get first-hand feedback.

How do you see the future of your segment of the industry?

It is the future! I think as a designer you have an obligation to consider what you are doing and why; ultimately we want to make strong, sustainable choices that provide our customers with a completely unique and desirable product. Many people are grappling with what the circular economy will really look like. I also believe that with technology there is a real opportunity to change things for good.

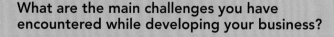

What are the main challenges you have encountered while developing your business?

Over ten years we've experienced every challenge normal to developing a small business, from cashflow and skills to space. Because of the nature of the REMADE business, sourcing and manufacturing challenges are daily headaches, but that's all part of the fun! A common challenge for sustainable brands is minimum order quantities for fully recycled materials. For young designers, it's even more tricky. The cost and implication of using recycled materials is generally 30 percent higher.

2. Brands, consumers, and trends

Learning objectives

- Find out how to define a brand
- Use research and visualization processes to develop strong customer profiles
- Comprehend the structure and use of trend research
- Be familiar with the purpose and practical application of fashion research

Defining a Brand

Designing is a challenging balance of creativity and strategic thinking. All brands must carry a clear message and present themselves to their audience in an intentional, understandable, and unique manner. In order to do so, companies must plan a specific direction before launching any new product, as anything the brand sells will need to embody this vision. While established companies usually focus on maintaining and reinforcing their existing **brand identity**, new design ventures must start with an active focus on branding. Effective brand design is an essential step for all start-up businesses, and relies on the combined analysis of marketplace dynamics and consumer behavior.

What is a niche?

Before determining the complete brand direction, designers and merchandisers must first identify a **niche** for their intended venture. A niche is a narrow placement within the marketplace, and is needed so that a company can appear unique to its consumers. Consider, for example, the denim market. While there are plenty of companies catering to this product area, each brand focuses on a specific segment of consumers, which provides a stronger sense of brand identity. Shoppers who identify with the brand image presented by Wrangler, for instance, are unlikely to respond positively to brands such as Emporio Armani or 7 for All Mankind. This produces a form of competitive strategy called **monopolistic competition**, in which each brand's purpose is to create the perception of uniqueness so it can act as a monopoly within its niche.

Right: True Religion have successfully created a niche market for themselves in premium denim.
Opposite: A runway show by Chanel, a globally recognized brand.

Burberry's key product, the trench coat, seen on actress Li Bingbing.

Selecting a product area

The starting point for determining a suitable niche is to identify the primary product upon which the brand will build its reputation. Obviously, most brands carry a variety of products, but virtually every brand in the marketplace was developed from a core product focus. Designer brands, such as Burberry and Chanel, present a broad assortment of looks each season, but are each synonymous with very specific garments, namely the Burberry trench coat and the Chanel tweed jacket. Accordingly, new designers and brands must first identify their intended product focus. Product areas may be defined by specific **apparel** categories, such as denim, knitwear, outerwear, or cocktail, as in the respective examples of Diesel, Sonia Rykiel, Moncler, and Elie Saab. Alternatively, a brand may choose to define its product area based on intended purpose, such as activewear, office, or leisure (as exemplified by Reebok, Reiss, and Levi's respectively). The challenge with focusing on the apparel's purpose is that such a choice can prove overly vague, and may require

additional clarification. Designers intending to launch a new brand should select their product area based on their talents and creative interests. Following the simple mantras "focus on what you are good at" and "do what makes you happy" greatly helps new brands to present innovative and exciting ideas in a crowded marketplace.

Discovering market openings

For a niche to provide suitable opportunities for a new business to grow, it must be currently unoccupied. Therefore, the second step in niche selection is to assess the offerings presented by competing brands within that chosen product area. Identification of possible segments of the marketplace that are not currently being catered to will form the basis for a valuable niche. These unexplored areas of the marketplace are usually referred to as **market openings**.

The practical way to identify such openings is to analyze existing brands using a narrow set of parameters. Evaluate them on a standardized rating system, according to criteria such as price, trendiness, creativity, technology, and so forth. Selecting the most effective criteria for this process depends on which of these will prove most important for the intended consumers. For example, if we focus on the designer-level marketplace for business tailoring, it is possible to place individual brands on a scale going from traditional to experimental. Brands such as Brunello Cucinelli, Oscar de la Renta, Alexander McQueen, and Vivienne Westwood would all sit at different levels on this scale. Segments of the scale that do not currently have brands associated with them indicate market openings. Of course, the effectiveness of this process rests in the thoroughness of the analysis. Doing this for only a handful of brands in a much larger marketplace would create false indications of potential market openings.

Vivienne Westwood tailoring **(left)** expresses very different brand values compared to the tailored work of Brunello Cucinelli **(above)**.

Brand values

Whether starting a new brand or designing for an existing business, brand values provide the basis for all design, promotional, and operational decisions. Each brand is guided by a series of core principles, which must connect to the personal values of the consumer it aims to target. While each value concept can be applied in absolute terms, it is most beneficial to consider each value statement in the context of the range between opposing principles.

The value ranges most often linked to fashion businesses include:

— Exclusivity – Approachability
— Luxury – Affordability
— Classicism – Creative innovation
— Formality – Casualness
— Quality – Trendiness
— Traditional – Technological
— Ethical – Cost-driven

Once a brand establishes its core values, these will drive brand direction, and remain consistent over time. Every brand therefore faces the daily dual challenge of creating innovative seasonal products and promotions, while remaining true to its primary brand message. Seasonal innovation is important to attract the attention of press, buyers, and consumers, but, without the esthetic continuity fostered by adherence to brand values, the collections would appear scattered and confusing. It is easy to see this dual challenge play out by observing various collections from a single design house, and identifying not only differences but also commonalities between seasons. The similarities are the visible result of a consistent focus on brand values.

To be effective contributors in this industry, all designers, marketing specialists, advertising executives, and social-media strategists must not only be able to understand the brand values of the company they work for, but – most importantly – to translate these values into products and images that will effectively communicate what the brand stands for with its intended consumers.

Store displays, like this elegant architectural space at the Victoria Beckham flagship store in London, are designed to attract consumers who will appreciate the brand's creative message.

Customer Profile

While driven by artistry and creative esthetic expression, any company in the fashion industry must generate enough sales to remain financially healthy, and must therefore create product that connects with its intended user. To do so effectively, it is essential to understand consumers in their constantly evolving social context. Prior to delving into consumer segmentation and the processes of **customer profiling**, let's define what **consumption** is.

From a simple economic standpoint, consumption refers to the act of buying goods or services. Fashion theory, however, goes further into understanding consumption as an act of identity-building. Every time we buy a piece of apparel or an accessory, we are ever so slightly changing who we appear to be. Each item of dress carries a symbolic value, in part defined by its functional shape, and in part by its brand and esthetic associations. By choosing to wear one item instead of another, consumers select how they are visually presenting themselves to the world. In this sense, consuming fashion is a lifestyle-driven process, and a constant dialog between personal expression and the individual's need to fit in with their social peers.

Consumer segmentation

Consumers are usually understood according to a series of research approaches, including demographics, psychographics, generational cohorts, and life stages. Each of these carries possible benefits and challenges, which leads to many fashion companies adopting a combined approach, making simultaneous use of more than one of these processes. Segmentation aims to divide a large population into smaller groups, which will be easier to understand and target by **manufacturers** and **retailers**. Approaches to consumer segmentation tend to center on either quantitative research (based on statistics and numbers) or qualitative research (based on ideas and opinions). The groupings are arrived at in the following ways.

Demographics are the "statistical characteristics of human populations," and these quantifiable data points – age, geographical location, ethnicity, income, education, and profession – are an important part of consumer segmentation. They can provide easy-to-understand groupings that share statistical similarities, but do not give much information regarding behavioral patterns, esthetic preferences, and decision-making processes.

Psychographics focus on qualitative analysis of consumer groups. This approach targets opinions, beliefs, values, and preferences, which are all very informative in understanding why consumers prefer certain products or brands.

Brands such as Prada draw in consumers with carefully planned visual merchandising.

Brands, consumers, and trends

Below and right: Consumer priorities vary greatly according to many factors such as age, occupation, interests, and values.
Bottom: Urban environments are a melting pot of diverse consumers, and provide great opportunities for brands to discover new market openings.

Multi-generational advertising, as in this Tommy Hilfiger campaign, aim to broaden the appeal of the brand.

Psychographics involve a more challenging process of research than traditional demographics and require more personal and time-consuming methods of data-gathering, such as interviews, focus groups, and questionnaires. Due to the nature of the information collected, the data can be harder to analyze.

Generational cohorts are groups of consumers whose patterns of behavior and consumer preferences have been identified according to the generation to which they belong (see chart below). Sociocultural events linked to the formative years of each generational cohort affect individuals' long-term patterns of consumption and social engagement. While this segmentation can provide some broad understanding of large segments of society, and

may help with planning business strategy in the long term, it does not offer much actionable information on the smaller scale.

Life stages aim to provide additional refinement of behavioral understanding beyond demographics (see chart on page 40). They explore how important personal events affect consumers' relationships with their social environments and with the consumption process itself. It can easily be understood how a consumer who is repaying college loans, owns a home, and has children will make very different choices than a person of the same age who does not have the same financial and familial obligations.

GENERATIONAL COHORT	Silent Generation	Baby Boomers	Generation X	Millennials	Gen Z
Born	1925–1945	c.1946–1964	c.1965–1979	c.1980–1995	c.1996–
Key behavioral traits	Dedicated to the common cause, strong sense of duty, loyalty, and sacrifice. Only purchase what they can afford or have saved for.	Distrusting of authority. Professionally highly competitive. First generation to buy goods on credit.	Skeptical, with a strong need for security. Motivated by money and self-reliant. Cautious spenders.	Tolerant, idealistic, and with a strong need for social connectedness. Financially dependent on parents longer than previous generations.	High levels of technological fluency. Natural entrepreneurs. Globally focused.

CONSUMER LIFE STAGES		
Life stage	Description	Priorities
Bachelorhood	Young and single.	Entertainment and recreation.
Honeymooners	Young couple, no children.	Experiences, real estate, home goods.
Parenthood 1	Young couple, infant to primary-school children.	Children's clothing, furniture, medical services, childcare.
Parenthood 2	Middle-aged parents with dependent children.	Education, food, clothing, entertainment.
Post parenthood	Older parents with dependent children.	Domestic help, higher education, luxury products, experiences.
Empty nest	Older parents with independent children.	Healthcare, security, value.
Solitary survivor	Old, retired singles.	Medical and legal services.

Customer visualization

Designers and all the creative teams they collaborate with must be able to understand and describe their target customer clearly and effectively. The best tool to achieve this is commonly referred to as a **customer profile**. While this may take several forms, whether a wall of loosely pinned images in a design studio, a page in a designer's **portfolio**, or a formal statement on the company website, its purpose is to identify the brand's target customer.

A visual approach to customer profiling is often most effective, as describing a customer exclusively in writing can sometimes result in vague or unclear statements. Regardless of approach, the first step is to list the main esthetic values of the intended consumer. Whenever listing values, being specific is of the utmost importance. Words such as "edgy" and "unique" are ambiguous, and can mean very different things to different people. Listing a consumer's core lifestyle values should therefore be a careful and insightful process.

Examples of effective esthetic value terminology

Imaginative Romantic Whimsical Profound Spiritual Expressive Erudite Resourceful Artistic "Woke" Assertive Practical Bashful Sociable Family-oriented Pop Humorous Flamboyant Changing Secretive Ambitious Personable Intimidating Playful Trendy

Once a selection of core esthetic values has been determined for the intended consumer, this handful of terms is used to seek out imagery that will visualize the person's lifestyle. Specificity is important. Each image will express slightly different interpretations of the search terms, so it is important to view enough options to bring the ideal representation of the intended consumer into focus. Imagery collected in this process generally includes:

Interiors: Consumers' personality expresses itself very visibly through the spaces they spend time in. Gather images of residential interiors (living rooms, family rooms, lofts, apartments, etc.) as well as public spaces (galleries, bars, restaurants, and museums).

Art: Like interiors, images of the kind of art that the consumer would find esthetically appealing can help to build an effective picture of their individual sense of **taste**.

Products/objects: While certain products might be too generic to contribute to the process of consumer visualization, directional products with specific visual character can be informative about the intended consumer's style preferences. For example, when visualizing a globe-trotter, include images of items collected on his or her travels. Carefully consider the unique value of the product being chosen.

Street style: This can be a very effective tool to visualize the intended consumer as a relatable person. **Editorial** photography should not be used for this, as it tends to be overly styled and removes many of the human qualities of its subjects. Rather, seek out candid shots of individuals who share the consumer's esthetic values.

Some common pitfalls in the process of profiling a target consumer include selecting imprecise or overly generic value terms or imagery. Types of visuals that would fall into this potentially problematic area are:

Generic cityscapes: Considering the number of people who live in places like New York City or London, a picture of their skyline does not provide much information about the specific customer being targeted.

Plain accessories, jewelry, and cosmetics: Items such as simple high heels, strings of pearls, and solitaire rings are used by a broad swathe of society, so are not informative enough for brand-specific consumer profiling.

Food and drink: Their functional nature tends to restrict images of food and drink from communicating esthetically.

Celebrities: Avoid using images of celebrities, as opinions on any public person differ so much. Basing a collection on a divisive celebrity can hinder the relatability of the work.

Once a suitably varied set of imagery has been collected, it must then be edited, organized, and composed in an elegant visual **layout** as a customer-profile board. Tips on effective

approaches to layout can be found in Chapter 7 (see page 172). The purpose of a customer-profile board is to bring the same understanding of the intended consumer to all creative-team members, promoters, stylists, and any other brand collaborators. For designers working on multiple collections simultaneously, or designers in training, being able to accurately visualize a consumer for each design project serves the valuable purpose of communicating their awareness of the commercial nature of the industry, and providing clear context for their creative work.

Top: Interiors offer great insight into consumers' style preferences.
Above: Street-style photography shows consumers expressing themselves through dress.
Left: The art that consumers like says a lot about their sense of style. This collage by Eugenia Loli conveys a clear sense of fun and whimsy.

The Thrill

Summer/Spring 2017

TOPSHOP

Melodi Isapoor

Consumer-profile digital collage by Melodi Isapoor.

Trend Research

While many people think of **trends** exclusively in terms of a popular color, silhouette, or detail, researching trends involves a much more inquisitive approach to social changes. A trend is in fact any change in popular taste or preference over time. Consequently, researching trends is primarily about understanding the causes and effects of a broader sociological evolution and how this comes to life through product choices.

This process of research is rather intricate, and relies on formal demographic and psychographic analysis, field observation, and the application of considerable creative intuition on the part of the analyst. Some **trend forecasting** companies have, over the years, built a very strong record of successful trend assessment and prediction, and have gained excellent reputations as reliable sources of direction for both brand strategy and design development. These leading forecasting companies include WGSN, Trendstop, Doneger, Peclers Paris, Trend Union, Promostyl, Edelkoort, Nelly Rodi, TOBE, and Fashion Snoops. Subscription to these services can be very expensive, but will also likely generate substantially higher sales for the company, so it can prove a valuable investment.

The trend-forecasting process

Most companies who research and forecast trends for the commercial marketplace follow a two-step process. First, they define **macrotrends**, and then determine how these will inform specific style forecasts. While each trend-research company collects and analyzes data according to distinctive processes, and presents unique insights based on their individual expertise, the ingredients that form the basis of trend research usually include two main components: media scans and observation of leading phenomena.

Media scans involve gathering large amounts of media content (newspapers, magazines, television, social media,

Above: Color forecasts on display at the Première Vision trade show.
Below: Street style in Milan.

Denim forecast at the Denim by Première Vision trade show.

etc.) and analyzing them according to standardized approaches. This helps to identify changes in the prevalence of key topics, as certain ideas gain or lose presence in the media, indicating a growth or shrinking of the associated trends. Media scans can be organized according to an individually selected series of research topics, but the most common structure of such research is illustrated by the acronym P.E.S.T.E.L., which stands for Political, Economic, Social, Technological, Environmental, and Legal. Obviously, none of these topics is fashion-specific, but changes in culture and consumer behavior can occur in all these areas, leading to the evolution of taste and therefore fashion.

Leading phenomena are occurrences that cannot be predicted through media scans. These happen without clear predictors, and can cause major upheavals in culture and consumer patterns. An example of a major leading phenomenon is the collapse of the lending industry in late 2008. The resulting stock-market crash, both in the United States and around the world, caused tangible repercussions on commercial markets, widening the gap between luxury brands and **budget** retailers. Observing leading phenomena requires being constantly abreast of news and events that may prove significant.

Macrotrends

The first product of trend research is focused on tracking large-scale, long-term changes in social preferences and behaviors, usually referred to as macrotrends (or megatrends). Macrotrends evolve over decades, and provide valuable insight for long-term strategic planning and business positioning. Trend forecasters therefore constantly track the evolution of these phenomena and adjust their forecasts accordingly. Over the decades, some widespread macrotrends have impacted consumer society in systemic ways. Below are some of the key macrotrends that continue to evolve and affect the fashion industry.

Hierarchic to casual: Modern society has been consistently moving away from traditional hierarchic structures. Casual clothing has simultaneously become increasingly acceptable in a variety of contexts. Examples of this can be seen in the growth of "casual Friday" dressing, which has gradually mutated into the everyday acceptability of casual business dressing in many workplaces. Similarly, the designer-level acceptance of athleisure is a symptom of this macrotrend.

BE CURIOUS. FIND OUT. DO SOMETHING

FASHION
REVOLUTION

fashionrevolution.org   @fash_rev

Top: Redefining gender on the runway. Look by Alessandro Trincone.
Above: The organization Fashion Revolution has actively promoted multicultural inclusiveness through their media campaigns.
Right: Blending active and traditional esthetics, an athleisure look by Valentino, Fall 2017.

Redefining gender roles: From the increasing acceptance of women in business leadership roles, to the growing acceptance in mass-media of non-binary gender expressions and non-traditional sexualities, the visual determination of gender roles has been evolving for the last century. This evolution is embodied in the recent work of, among others, Gucci and Thom Browne.

From local to global: The economic interconnectedness of global markets has led to cultural interconnectedness. Awareness of and engagement with cultures worldwide has radically redefined where fashion comes from. A style that may appear in Seoul can immediately be popularized worldwide through a multitude of platforms, a process that would have been inconceivable as recently as the 1990s.

Technology as a way to connect: While technology served a functional, productive purpose until the second half of the 20th century, inventions such as the fax machine, the cell phone, and, most importantly, the introduction of the Internet in the mid-1990s have all been focused on enhancing the ability of humans to connect. This focus on personal connection and human relationships will continue to express itself in future technological innovations, as it has in such items as the Apple watch or the Nike+ line of connected footwear.

Ethical living: While the principle of environmentalism can be traced back to the beginning of the 20th century, it has taken a broader multifaceted form over time. Ethical concerns are now guiding the products and services of brands from Stella McCartney to H&M.

Style forecasting

Once the evolution of macrotrends is established, the next step is to expand these core directions into more specific, individually focused, and product-driven trend paths. This is where the contribution of expert panels, specialist color forecasters, or material consultants can be of particular value. In this process, new colors, silhouettes, details, or fabrics are predicted by forecasting companies because they effectively reflect the projected change in social preferences. This is usually established much closer to the season being envisaged. While macrotrend forecasts can take place two or more years in advance, these style trends (also referred to as short-term trends or microtrends) are usually published only about one year beforehand.

Some common patterns to be aware of when considering short-term trend patterns concern the trend path and tempo. Understanding these common patterns can provide a valuable tool in foreseeing the possible evolution of any given trend. Virtually all short-term trends can be understood in relationship to one of these path patterns:

Trickle-down trends start at the luxury level, then become imitated by mid-tier and mass-market brands. Most often, this pattern can be applied to trends that involve traditionally luxury-focused objects or styles, but may also stem from an avant-garde style shown on the catwalk. Trends such as the use of rococo **embroidery**, **laser-cut** surfaces, or formal evening wear are good examples of this pattern.

Bubble-up trends start in subcultural groups, such as punk, goth, emo, and Lolita. Individuals in these groups choose to dress differently from the norm in order to express their divergence from the prevailing philosophical view of the world. When the styles developed by these youth subcultures become the source of inspiration for established designers and mainstream brands, this is considered a bubble-up trend path.

Below left: From court dress to ready-to-wear: trickle-down trends on display at Dolce&Gabbana.
Below center: This collection by Balmain incorporates extensive street-style references, an example of a bubble-up trend.
Below right: Fast-fashion retailers such as H&M construct their business model on trickle-across trends.

THE ADOPTION OF INNOVATION CURVE

FADS, FASHIONS, AND CLASSICS

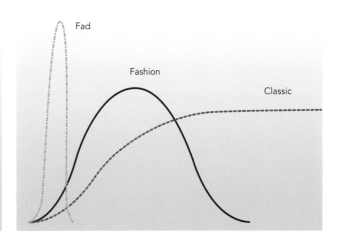

Trickle-across trends arise in any part of the world and at any level of the marketplace, to become instantly diffused through all levels of the industry. This is thanks to global improvements in mass-communication, production, and distribution. Deciding which styles become virally diffused is in the hands of individuals called **gatekeepers**, who include powerful editors, buyers, and retailers. The role of these fashion decision-makers is therefore to sift through enormous amounts of options and handpick the few trends that will become meaningful for the season to come. Fast-fashion brands operate in this way.

Style trends can also be analyzed based on the tempo or timeframe of their evolution. All trends that gain reasonably popular acceptance present a pattern that looks like a bell shape and is called the adoption of innovation curve (see graph above). The beginning of the bell indicates the introduction of the trend, where only innovators are engaging with it. Quickly thereafter, early adopters join the trend, leading to visible growth in the curve. Once enough early adopters display the style, there is a chain reaction in which the majority are now suitably assured of the reasonable viability of the trend, and will start adopting it as well. The end of the curve indicates the fading out of the trend, and is populated by a social group called laggards, who tend to adopt new trends out of necessity or lack of other options.

This process, leading from innovators to laggards, can take place at fast or slow speeds, leading to the different tempo-based paths below.

Classics: A style that is introduced, gains visibility, reaches mass-acceptance, and then does not fade away is known as a classic. While denim jeans first appeared in key street

styles in the 1950s, they did not become widely popular until the 1960s, when they became associated with anti-war demonstrations. Over the following decade, jeans evolved into an accepted everyday style, and have not lost their prevalence since.

Fashions: A fashion usually evolves over the course of one to three years. Trends such as metallics, pixelated prints, and double-breasted jackets come in and out of popularity on a path that takes several months from early onset to final rejection. Over the course of this time, the trend will go from a handful of style leaders to broad-majority acceptance, and finally fade out.

Fads: These trends are short-lived but very intense. Fads are most likely to be targeted at teenage consumers, who are more prone to value temporary popularity. British Knights sneakers in 1990, Tamagotchi in the late 1990s, and fidget spinners in 2017 are all examples of fads.

Designers and merchandisers often state that all trends are cyclical. While this may be somewhat of an exaggeration, a certain repetitiveness of style appears to be visible in modern decades. There is a technical difference between cyclical trends and trends known as long-wave phenomena. While both refer to recurring styles or esthetic codes, cyclical trends are defined as regularly recurring patterns that achieve the same level of acceptance each time they take place. This is quite a strict set of parameters to meet, and is therefore extremely rare. By contrast, a long-wave phenomenon refers to any trend that, while showing a repetitive nature, may change tempo or intensity. An example of a long-wave phenomenon would be the repeated stylistic referencing of ancient Grecian dress that occurred in Imperial Rome (c.1st century BCE),

during the Italian Renaissance (c.15th century CE), the Neoclassical period (c.1800–20), and then repeatedly in the 20th century in the work of Mariano Fortuny, Madeleine Vionnet, Alix Grès, Donna Karan, and many others. Each time the style repeated, it was somewhat altered and reached a different section of the population, making it not a pure cyclical trend, but a long-wave pattern.

Designers and merchandisers must be well versed in the terminology and functional structure of trend research, as their work is in itself predictive. Due to the extensive time it takes to develop, produce, and distribute apparel items, designers are likely to be working on fashion seasons one full year in advance. In this context, being able to exploit the predictive tools through a core appreciation of trend research can lead to more commercially successful design decisions.

Above: Blue jeans, a classic style globally popularized by iconic films such as *Rebel Without a Cause*, 1955, starring James Dean.
Right: Grecian-style dresses, like this 1950s Alix Grès look, are reinterpreted each time they reappear in style, making them a long-wave phenomenon.

Fashion Research

While trend research aims to predict the future of style, fashion research is primarily focused on understanding its present. Fashion companies more or less use fashion research based on the type of design philosophy they follow, and while **design imitators** and **interpreters** may use fashion research quite prolifically, this is rarely the case for true fashion innovators (see discussion of design philosophies on page 24). Fashion research is, in essence, an applied form of competitive research. By researching what is currently on the market, what has recently been shown by competing brands, and how magazines are promoting certain styles over others, designers can better ensure that their work will resonate with the current taste dominating their segment of the industry.

Fashion research does not predict the future; rather, it identifies the present status of the industry, so it is substantially different from trend forecasts. Similarly, this type of research presents information on styles and looks that are already on the market, and are therefore not suitable sources of creative inspiration for original **design innovator** exploration.

Any designer basing their creative process on fashion research would essentially be working about six months behind schedule, causing their work to feel outdated. The only obvious exception to this general rule is visible in fast fashion, where imitators thrive by copying existing styles and bringing them to consumers even faster than the designer brands being imitated.

Fashion research has three primary components, each of which provides certain unique insights and opportunities: runway reports, editorial research, and shopping the market.

Fashion research in leading boutiques such as this Trussardi store can inform design, styling, and merchandising strategies.

Runway reports can identify commercial trends in the market, such as this "tropical floral" vibe visible in the same season across multiple runways, including Dries van Noten **(left)** and Mary Katrantzou **(below)**.

Runway reports

As the name suggests, runway reports focus on providing a synopsis of recent runway shows, identifying key directions, styles, silhouettes, colors, details, and so on. Compiling an effective runway report can be quite time-consuming, and requires an elevated ability to recognize patterns and connections across a vast amount of visual information.

Runway reporting starts with either attending as many shows as possible or gathering images from a variety of shows relevant to the market segment. The analysis will then consist in generating groupings guided by visual similarities. These groupings may be focused on certain materials, **construction** elements, use of color, mood, or any other connection between pieces from various collections. The key is to identify how the work of multiple designers may be aligning in some way. These areas of cohesion are likely to become relevant retail trends, as runway reports are often the primary tool used by buyers and retailers when deciding which products to purchase and how to present them in-store.

Many trend-forecasting companies, such as WGSN, provide runway-reporting services alongside their forecasting information.

Editorial research

This type of research focuses on gathering an overview of editorial material from a broad variety of fashion publications. An "editorial" refers to a photograph or series of photographs that has been styled and shot in ways that are more focused on storytelling and mood than communicating the details and construction of the garment itself. Magazines such as *Vogue*, *i-D*, *Popeye's*, and *WestEast* spend a lot of time and resources creating unique editorial photoshoots, showcasing meaningful retail trends for the upcoming season. The challenge of editorial research is to garner enough variety of material to get a broad perspective on the current esthetic language being promoted by fashion editors in their role as gatekeepers.

For designers and merchandisers, being able to employ esthetic choices in their work that align with those of leading fashion editors can enhance the work's acceptance by these industry gatekeepers, and in turn translate into heightened sales.

Editorial photographs published in magazines and online give information not only about specific garments, but also the mood and style that are currently in vogue. *W* magazine, Korea.

Shopping the market

The final component of fashion research requires some physical engagement. Shopping the market is, as the name suggests, the process of physically visiting competing stores. The lead creative teams of many brands will regularly go to the retail locations of their competitors in order to gain deeper understanding of how these other brands are merchandising their stores and presenting themselves to their customers.

Evidently, this is a clear and direct form of competitive analysis aimed at ensuring that a brand's creative strategy, in terms of design, merchandising, and visual communication, are better than their competitors'.

Some aspects of shopping the market may be accessible digitally. Companies such as WindowsWearPro specialize in garnering up-to-date images of store windows and interiors, and sharing these with their subscribers in real time. While such digital information can be valuable, the insight gained by personally visiting the competition's stores is much more meaningful, as it will provide not only the visual aspects of the venue, but also an understanding of how consumers connect and interact with the space and product.

Visiting retail venues such as the Balmain store **(opposite)** or a streetwear boutique **(below)** offers insights into the garments being sold, the product assortment being offered, and the broader merchandising and branding approach; how the store feels often becomes more important than what the store carries.

Designer Profile: Eudon Choi

Eudon Choi is the creative director of his eponymous label.

Tell us about what made you want to be a designer.

My grandmother, mother, and sister were all very into fashion, which definitely influenced me. My grandmother had boutiques before I was born. She had such incredible fashion sense it was hard not to be affected.

I was always drawing as a child, but I first knew I wanted to be a designer when I came across the shoot 'Grunge and Glory' by Steven Meisel in American *Vogue* 1992.

There was a sense of individuality and personal style that radiated from model Kristen McMenamy. The clash of sources and new wave of style felt like something I wanted to be a part of.

How would you describe your brand?

I'd describe EUDON CHOI as masculine tailoring with a feminine sensibility. I have a background in menswear design, so I always focus on using sartorial techniques and

masculine cuts to shape the female form. I love hiding menswear detailing in womenswear, and including things like a coin pocket in jackets.

I find inspiration in art, architecture, and history. I like to reinterpret and reference others' creative journeys in my own. My AW18 collection was based on a collective of artists in the harbor town of St Ives [in Cornwall, England]. I looked at the naive artist Alfred Wallis and paid homage to the fishermen and miners who also worked there.

Why did you choose your specific niche? What opportunities has it provided you?

Being a London-based Korean designer has provided me with more opportunities than I could ever have imagined. I feel very lucky to live here and be embraced as a designer. It's such an amazing city; known for its diversity and innovation, it really gives me the freedom to be playful. As a city, it incubates young talent like no other, and the support from the British Fashion Council is really amazing.

The London woman is totally unique. I love to design pieces that marry into her wardrobe.

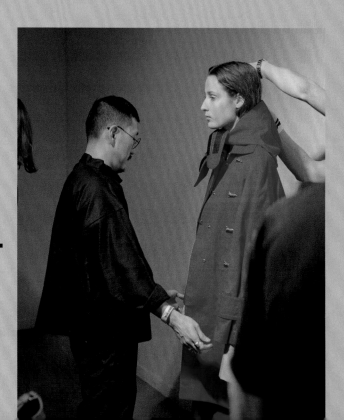

How do your chosen customer and market influence your design approach?

I feel my collections only come alive when they have reached the customer. I design pieces that fit with their wardrobes and I love to see how they style them and make them their own.

It's so rewarding to see my vision realized in that sense. I have a very close relationship with my customers and am always listening to what they want and how I can improve their fashion experience.

I want my customer to keep the pieces in their wardrobe for a long time, revisit them, and keep falling back in love with them. I like to think that women come to me for their wardrobe staples, investment pieces that can be worn again and again. My pieces are classic with a twist.

What are the main challenges you have encountered while developing your business?

The biggest challenge I find is to have a balance between creativity and commerciality. For a young label it's important to offer something new, but it's equally important to grow the business and survive in the industry.

There are so many labels that come and go, I'm very grateful to still be here and showcasing nine years on.

How do you see the future of your segment of the industry?

No one could have predicted how social media and Instagram could have had such an influence on the industry, so who knows what the future could hold? I like to think that the future of fashion is in sustainability. I'd love to find ways to recycle more in the fashion industry.

3. Inspiration and research

Learning objectives

- Understand the various types of concepts used in fashion design

- Appreciate brainstorming as a tool to bridge concept inspiration and visual research

- Understand the process of research planning

- Be familiar with various tools and approaches for gathering research

- Explore strategies and techniques for the creation of original research

- Identify considerations and frameworks used to establish a strong color story

- Examine the challenges of material sourcing in developing a fashion collection

Concept and Ideation

The establishment of an effective **concept** direction is a necessary step in preparing to move toward effective design development. Concepts can take many forms and play an essential role not only in guiding the creative process, but also in communicating the value and innovativeness of the final product to consumers.

Well-known designers tend to employ a consistent approach to concept-building, which becomes an integral part of their creative signature and **brand identity**. This chapter introduces the various types of concept that designers and **product developers** may embrace, as well as the steps required to expand this initial direction into a complete body of research that will foster design exploration.

What is a concept?

The word "concept" is often used to signify a multitude of possible forms of inspiration. There is common ground behind the various meanings of this word: it is a source of creative fuel, a guiding force that stands as the foundation of all steps of collection and brand development.

Conceptual direction creates a foundation not only for designs, but also for styling, visual merchandising, press communication, and consumer engagement. With this in mind, it is important to understand that designers benefit greatly from a clear and intentional approach. Building a fashion collection is a group effort involving collaboration with textile designers, accessory designers, pattern-makers, stylists, and PR consultants, to name but a few. The more designers are able to clearly articulate and communicate their creative inspiration, the more effectively their team will work together in purposeful unison.

Above: Mood board backstage at Salvatore Ferragamo, Milan.
Opposite: Horses Design studio: a designer in front of her inspiration wall.

RESEA

Above: Mood board at Lucio Vanotti fashion show, at Pitti Uomo 90.
Right: Presenting many images in a portfolio format can be a challenge.
In such cases, it is useful to compile a brief visual synopsis of the key
research and theme, as in this concept board by Ariana Arwady.

Ways in to inspiration

Creative inspiration can come from a multitude of
sources, but generally conceptual approaches fall
within three main categories.

Narrative themes: This type of concept is used by
designers who create their collections based on a
storytelling process. The design development process
is driven primarily by objects, art, photography, **vintage**
garments, and other visual material connected to the story
being explored. Designers who follow this approach to
concept and inspiration tend to develop work that plays
with the intersection between costume and fashion. Such
designers include Alexander McQueen, John Galliano
(during his tenure as creative director of Dior), Thom
Browne, and many others.

Lifestyle inspiration: Designers can focus their creative
process by looking at the lifestyle of their customers. This
type of inspiration often centers upon an influential figure
referred to as a **muse**, who embodies the lifestyle being
explored. Design brands such as Tommy Hilfiger, COS, and
Giorgio Armani have consistently adopted this creative
approach. Concentrating on lifestyle inspiration can have
both positive and negative effects. While it strengthens
brand messaging with regard to the brand's proposed
consumer base, it can at times lead to repetitive designs
that lack innovation.

Conceptual design: This approach to creative inspiration
focuses on questioning how the design process works.
By investigating the standard ways of designing and
manufacturing, conceptual designers propose unique and
innovative approaches that translate into either artistic
statements unhindered by commercial concerns, or into
new solutions for the future of the **apparel** industry. The
products resulting from conceptual approaches can often
appear radically new, even at times offputtingly so, and
often contribute to avant-garde design esthetics. Designers
such as Martin Margiela, Rei Kawakubo, and Issey Miyake
consistently employ this approach to design inspiration.

Conceptual designs, like this Marina Hoermanseder look, do not usually derive from visual research, but instead from process-based thinking.

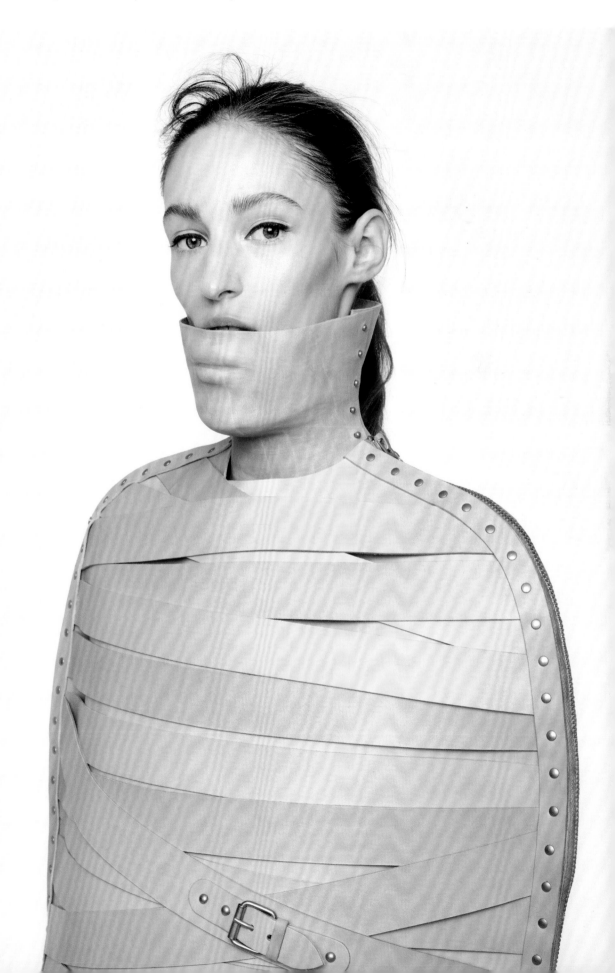

Case study

Narrative inspiration in Alexander McQueen, Spring 2010

The Spring 2010 collection by Alexander McQueen, entitled "Plato's Atlantis," was a masterpiece of narrative design. As the title suggests, it focused on the fantastical lost city of Atlantis, said to have been the site of an ancient, technologically advanced society, which was consumed by the ocean. Popular culture commonly links the city of Atlantis with alien civilization. These narrative paths formed the basis for the entire collection, from textiles and silhouettes to accessories and styling.

Color palette: This extensive collection explored several color groups. Colors evolve from reptilian coppers and bronze toward underwater blue–green hues, sea kelp, science-fiction grays, and laminated blacks.

Textiles and materials: McQueen's approach to material development in this collection was truly spectacular. Dozens of diverse prints, **embroideries**, and embellishments all played with the visual appearance of snakes, fish, mollusks, and ocean waves alongside abstracted references to alien technology and space travel.

Silhouettes: The explorations of silhouette in this collection showcased McQueen's creative draping techniques. The garments were constructed in sculptural volumes, reminiscent of seashells and spacecraft.

Styling: The narrative inspiration for the collection was strongly communicated in the styling of the show.

Accessories, hair and makeup, and overall collection presentation all contributed to this storytelling effort.

Accessories: These radically pushed the boundaries of their esthetic and functional purposes. Some shoes employed cast volumes, recalling the designs (originally created by H.R. Giger) of the creature from the *Alien* movies. Other shoes extended the leg into an unnaturally shaped extremity, providing further other-worldly appeal to their wearer.

Hair and makeup: Both of these were developed in ways to enhance the science-fiction esthetic. The models' faces were enhanced with prosthetics to make their appearance harder and more angular. Their hair was predominantly arranged in solidly sculpted, horn-like extensions, elongating their cranium vertically and backward, again achieving an alien-like esthetic.

The show was presented on a sleek white runway, framed on each side by mechanically automated arms each carrying a video camera, which enhanced the science-fiction vibe of the entire show. This narrative was reinforced by an original video, commissioned for the show, and displayed on the backdrop as an introduction to the collection. The video combined reptilian and organic textures in hypnotic kaleidoscopic pattern variations in tones of electric blue.

By analyzing this collection, it is evident that narratively inspired designers achieve strong results when the thematic concept at the core of their collection imbues every aspect of their work, from surface to shape, from product to styling.

Digital collage of the narrative inspiration behind the Alexander
McQueen Spring 2010 collection.

The stylistic elements of art deco, characterized by sharp geometry, streamlining, and rich materials, are highly visible both in the style of Chanel and in the design of the atrium of the Chrysler Building, New York City. Art deco was a lifestyle trend, lasting from the 1920s to the 1940s, which affected all areas of design.

Case study

Lifestyle inspiration in the work of Coco Chanel

Chanel's entire body of work was not inspired by a narrative or conceptual approach, but by her insight into women's lives. Chanel grew up in the *belle époque*, in a world before World War I where women wore corsets, cumbersome dresses, and large ornate hats. She knew society around her was changing rapidly, and so was the position of women within it. Urbanization, women striving for the right to vote, and entering the workplace in larger numbers than ever before, all meant that the impractical styles Chanel grew up with would soon become obsolete. Instead of promoting the old, aristocratic-inspired visions of luxury, Chanel made it her life's mission to dress the new modern woman.

Because of this focus on functionality, practicality, and esthetic simplicity, her work appears to be very consistent across the decades during which she designed. Her approach to color, silhouette, garment **construction**, and detailing were not exactly seasonal; they were part of a singular brand message, a message intended to express how her target customer lived her life. If you look at garments she designed in the 1920s alongside outfits created in the 1950s and 1960s, they appear virtually interchangeable. Subdued color palettes, flatteringly tubular soft volumes, and understatedly luxurious textures are the consistent hallmarks of her style.

Chanel's work foresaw many of the elements of contemporary womenswear today, including women wearing menswear-inspired tailored jackets and pants, or activewear-inspired styles.

Chanel's great contribution to 20th-century fashion was creating a new style of dressing that gave fashion consumers not just what they knew they wanted, but what they didn't know they needed. In this context, it is important to understand that the most successful approach to lifestyle-focused designing is not based on merely replicating what is already in the fashion marketplace, but on anticipating the unique needs of a changing society.

"Fashion is not something that exists only in dresses. Fashion is in the sky, in the street, fashion has to do with ideas, the way we live, what is happening." **Coco Chanel**

Garments by Issey Miyake, such as these three looks from his Fall 2016 collection, are not designed from visual inspiration, but through technological experimentation.

Case study

Conceptualism in the work of Issey Miyake

Each designer driven by a conceptual approach develops a unique process, sometimes referred to as **design methodology**, which greatly impacts the look of their work.

Embracing a conceptual approach means the designs take shape through the processes involved, and do not usually result from the traditional method of **croquis** sketching. The products instead take shape in unexpected ways, which leads to uniquely non-traditional outcomes.

The work of Issey Miyake is a perfect example of conceptual inspiration. Miyake has devoted his entire career to researching the boundaries of apparel production, particularly focusing on the ways in which new technology could radically impact the future of the fashion industry. He has consistently championed new fibers and materials and, most importantly, has worked in direct collaboration with engineers to develop pleating, weaving, and knitting machines that would allow him to create garments in new ways. His best-known ventures in this

conceptual exploration are commercialized under the labels Pleats Please and A-POC.

Pleats Please is a line ideated and produced through the use of specially designed pleating machinery. Garments are cut in simple geometric shapes and constructed in breathable, synthetic woven fabrics. The unfitted, tunic-like items are then put through a pleating process, which generates permanent fine creases in the fabric and alter the garments' fit, movement, and overall appearance. It is, in fact, the machine that gives the garments their final appearance and fit in ways that at times defy the esthetic norms of traditional fashion.

A-POC (the initial letters of "a piece of cloth") is the result of advanced research into knitting and weaving technology. Working with engineering specialists, Miyake developed new machinery able to knit and weave multiple layers of material simultaneously, and through that process to connect these layers together in certain predetermined areas. The resulting material, which exits the machine as an unassuming roll of fabric, can be cut apart and worn with no need for any sewing or additional construction. Once again, the fit and ultimate look of the garment are not the result of traditional **fashion sketching**, but instead result from the capabilities of the machinery itself, and the interactive involvement of the garment's actual user.

Brainstorming

Regardless of the type of concept being explored, whether narrative, lifestyle-focused, or process-driven, designers need to ensure that the initial idea is expanded in the broadest possible variety of creative directions. This broadening of the central concept is usually executed through a brainstorming or mind-mapping exercise.

Just as industrial designers produce "exploded views" of their designs to show each individual component that will make up the final product, so fashion designers need to explode their inspiration to find a wide range of individual elements that make up creative ideas, which can then be played with through the design-development phase.

Brainstorming should be based on the premise that it will inform a fashion collection. As such, it is beneficial to keep to the elements that will be investigated through the design process. These include:

— Mood/attitude/feeling
— Color
— Texture/surface/pattern
— Silhouette/shape
— Construction details
— Styling

The next step is to create a **mind map** (see opposite). Start by writing the core concept as a proposed collection title or short phrase in the center of a page, and placing the six areas of design focus listed above around it. Each area of the mind map should then be filled with a multitude of terms indicating options to consider during design development. All terms included in the brainstorming session should be connected to the central concept, while outlining a broad array of possibilities. It is important to keep in mind that a full fashion collection presented on the runway is often composed of 35–50 outfits, each of which is likely made up of multiple garments. The breadth of exploration at the brainstorming stage will enhance the variety and creative interest of the completed line.

Filling in each of the above sections of the brainstorming map relies on self-reflection – drawing on personal experience and memory – as well as external research, so additional options can evolve out of initial thoughts.

Some designers brainstorm more effectively by employing a sound-recording device, and documenting free-flowing word associations, which can then be transcribed to paper. As the brainstorming process is grounded in the creative use of terminology and language, making use of a thesaurus can be highly beneficial, but, when doing so, designers must ensure that they clearly understand the meaning of the words selected.

When composing the brainstorming map, figures of speech such as metaphor, personification, simile, onomatopoeia, and dissonance, can help in growing the list of options for each of the core areas of design focus. In addition, referencing the work of artists, photographers, filmmakers, and other creative professionals outside the field of fashion can lead to more imaginative **design experimentation** later on. Relying too heavily on current fashion references often leads to an **ideation** process that becomes overly derivative, and overly dependent on imitation instead of originality and creativity.

Precision of language and clarity of intent are paramount; when brainstorming color, "cerulean" or "periwinkle" are far more useful than "blue." Similarly, when mapping out silhouette possibilities, designers should refrain from vague terminology such as "classy" or "elegant."

The brainstorming session will form the foundation for all the design exploration to follow, from sourcing and selecting **fabrications** to exploring garment construction, and from visualizing color to planning the final styling of the line in **editorial** shoots or **portfolio** presentation. The importance of this process cannot be overstated.

A BRAINSTORMING MIND MAP

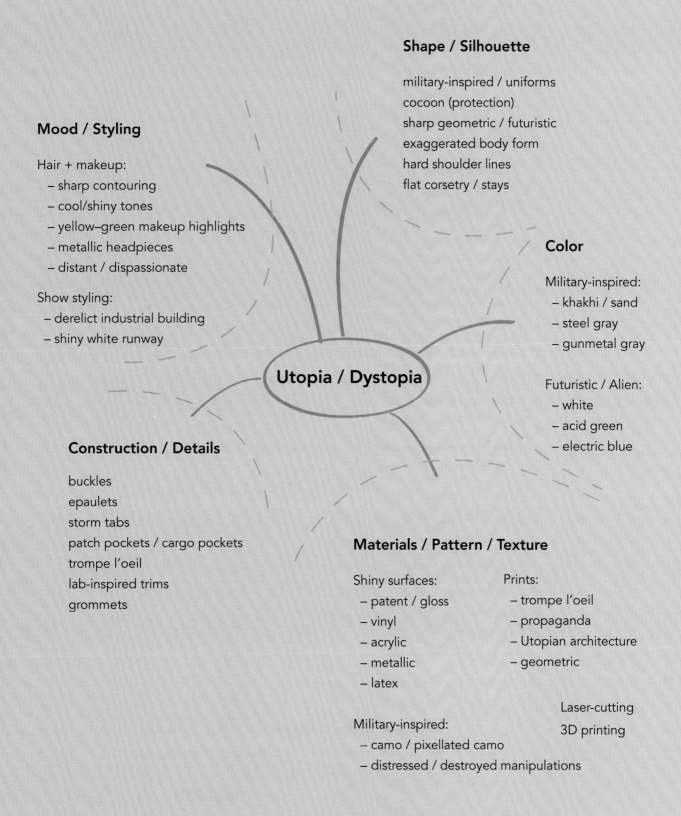

Shape / Silhouette

military-inspired / uniforms
cocoon (protection)
sharp geometric / futuristic
exaggerated body form
hard shoulder lines
flat corsetry / stays

Mood / Styling

Hair + makeup:
  – sharp contouring
  – cool/shiny tones
  – yellow–green makeup highlights
  – metallic headpieces
  – distant / dispassionate

Show styling:
  – derelict industrial building
  – shiny white runway

Color

Military-inspired:
  – khakhi / sand
  – steel gray
  – gunmetal gray

Futuristic / Alien:
  – white
  – acid green
  – electric blue

Utopia / Dystopia

Construction / Details

buckles
epaulets
storm tabs
patch pockets / cargo pockets
trompe l'oeil
lab-inspired trims
grommets

Materials / Pattern / Texture

Shiny surfaces:
  – patent / gloss
  – vinyl
  – acrylic
  – metallic
  – latex

Prints:
  – trompe l'oeil
  – propaganda
  – Utopian architecture
  – geometric

Laser-cutting
3D printing

Military-inspired:
  – camo / pixellated camo
  – distressed / destroyed manipulations

Research Planning

After completing a thorough brainstorming from the initial concept or theme, designers carry out extensive visual research, which is collected and explored, and which forms the basis for more direct design development and **visualization**.

Different forms of research should be employed to best guide design ideation, including **secondary research** (gathered from pre-existing sources) and **primary research** (your own investigative work). Some design approaches focus more on secondary research, while others rely almost exclusively on primary inquiry, which involves creating new content. Regardless of the prevalence of each type of research, designers start by planning out the steps and time required to amass all required information.

Collecting research, be it primary or secondary, can entail trips to museums, libraries, fashion-forward neigborhoods, trade shows, and historical places either locally or internationally, so it might require substantial time and financial resources. The material gathered is necessary to the development of the designs that will ultimately form the collection, so all research should be completed before starting garment ideation.

As a general rule, all research should be carried out within 10 percent of the total design-development timeline. The duration of the research is therefore in direct correlation to the overall time available. Traditional brands showing two full collections a year spend about ten weeks generating the designs for each line, while the remaining time is allocated to creating a **muslin prototype** (toile) and sample development. This means all relevant research for each of those collections is usually completed within the first seven days of the project. Design students are likely to work on smaller collection assignments, designing a final range of six to eight looks over the course of an academic term, but the same scheduling rule should be applied.

A common mistake, which can impact all subsequent design-development stages, occurs when designers fail to commit to an allocated timeframe for research. This may cause the collection ideation stages to be unnecessarily shortened, often leading to less inventive and original design results.

Complex projects are best organized by setting up a clear master calendar, which will help keep all team members on track.

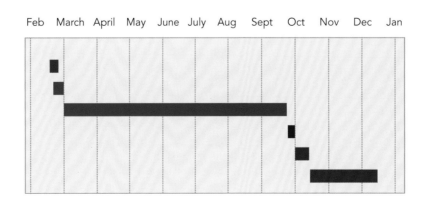

	Feb	March	April	May	June	July	Aug	Sept	Oct	Nov	Dec	Jan
Task												
Concept / research												
Fabric sourcing												
Design / prototyping												
Market week												
Pre-production												
Production												

FLOWCHART OF THE RESEARCH PROCESS

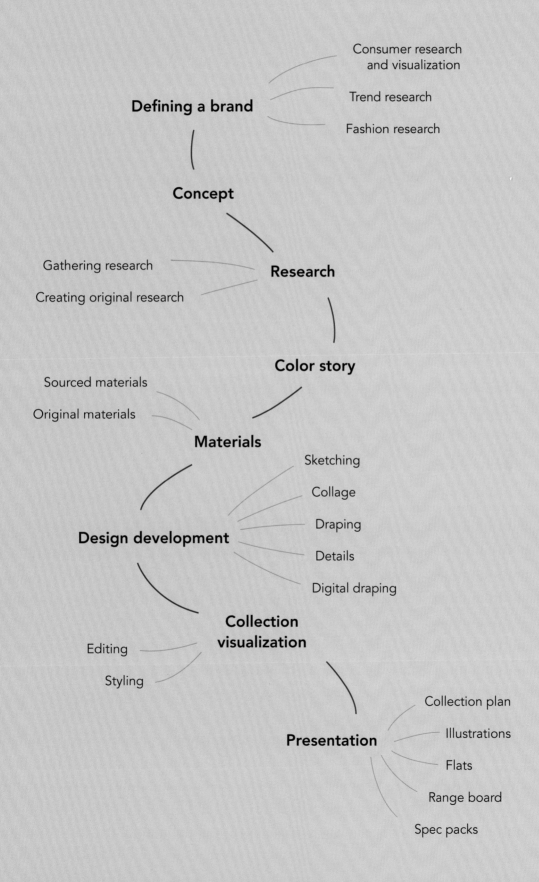

Defining a brand
- Consumer research and visualization
- Trend research
- Fashion research

Concept

Research
- Gathering research
- Creating original research

Color story

Materials
- Sourced materials
- Original materials

Design development
- Sketching
- Collage
- Draping
- Details
- Digital draping

Collection visualization
- Editing
- Styling

Presentation
- Collection plan
- Illustrations
- Flats
- Range board
- Spec packs

Gathering Research

Somewhat counterintuitively, secondary research usually occurs before primary research in the context of academic research projects. However, designers often combine secondary and primary processes (gathering content and creating content respectively) in a speedy research exploration.

Photography and art images often dominate secondary research, as they tend to be easier to implement directly into the design process. Visual content can be translated intuitively into design options and garment ideas through a variety of approaches discussed in Chapter 5 (see pages 114–141).

Written material, such as poetry, song lyrics, and novels may also provide valuable inspiration for designers, and should be gathered as part of this research step when relevant to the concept or theme being explored. Collecting written research will likely require a process of visualization or abstraction in order for the creative value of the research to become applicable to the design process. This visualization or abstraction step is a type of primary research process, and is therefore discussed in more depth on page 75.

Library research

Books, monographs, periodicals, magazines, and other publications are the main sources of gathered research. While many designers build a personal library of inspirational books over their careers, which they refer to time and again, they also plan research trips to local libraries at the start of each collection. This allows them to collect an ample selection of exciting images from materials relevant to their chosen theme or concept. It is important to note that much of the creative inspiration contained in books and other publications is not usually available online. Libraries can also offer interesting opportunities for unexpected discoveries. While browsing the shelves, the researcher may come across books or magazines that were not included in the original research plan, but that might present valuable content for developing the project. Such is the benefit of a hands-on

The inspiration board for Mary Katrantzou's Spring/Summer 2018 show, mixing a variety of collected imagery, original research, and fabric inspiration.

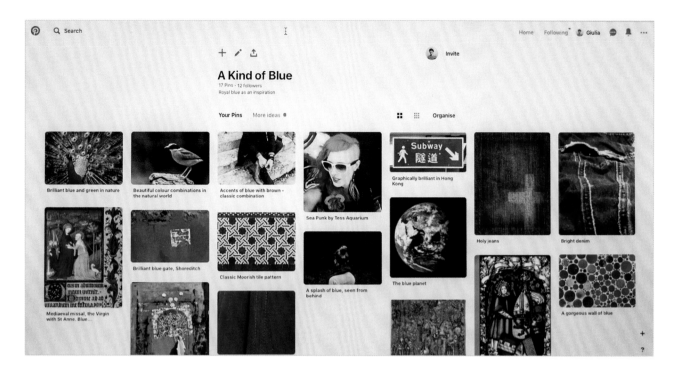

Social-media platforms such as Pinterest can be useful in exploring and recording visual research.

approach to secondary research; it can greatly enhance the uniqueness and creative value of the materials being gathered, and the ultimate design outcome.

Internet and social-media research

The amount of information we are able to summon nowadays online and on our smartphones can be quite overwhelming, and requires a keen critical eye to ensure its quality and relevance. When coming across images of research through digital channels, designers must always ask themselves the following questions:

Is this image at a sufficient resolution that I can use it?

Most images online are deliberately very small, with a screen resolution of 72 dpi/ppi, which makes them easier to share digitally. Images that are small and at screen **resolution** (72 dpi/ppi) are not usable for design development and presentation because, once printed, they will appear blurry or pixelated. This is an obvious technical problem that can heavily detract from the overall appeal of the design project being developed. Images gathered through digital channels should be at a printable size with a high resolution of 300 dpi/ppi. While some

search engines, such as Google Images, allow users to limit results based on overall image size, many do not. Gathering visual content through accredited databases such as WGSN, ARTstor, or the *Vogue* Archive can ensure the material gathered meets this need for high resolution.

Is this image esthetically relevant to my theme or concept?

Digital resources for visual research, including Google Images, Pinterest, Instagram, and others, present their users with a large selection of images based on their internal algorithmic logic. Algorithms are best described as mathematical formulae that edit content based on how many "likes" images have received, and on the individual user's search history. This means that these platforms tend to showcase the most popular content, or content that best matches previous selections. This, in turn, leads to digital searches resulting in the most predictable outcomes, with no consideration for artistic value or innovation. Researchers collecting visual material through digital platforms must therefore ensure that the images selected are meeting the esthetic needs of the project. Since designing fashion is about innovation and creativity, it should be fueled by visual research capable of fostering such thinking.

Above: Art can be a valuable source of creative information in terms of shape, volume, color, and mood. *Untitled* by Lesley Vance (2013).
Right: So many fashions follow a cyclical structure. Classic movies such as 1963's *Charade* provide useful direction about styles of the past.

Key sources of research

A variety of sources are commonly used in the process of gathering research. Each type listed below has challenges as well as potential benefits, so it is essential to understand its value and possible pitfalls.

Art: The visual language of fashion and the esthetic expression of art are inherently intertwined, so designers often seek inspiration from the output of painters, sculptors, performance artists, street artists, photographers, and other artists.

Since art is a creative expression of social meaning, it can help to connect fashion design to a more advanced esthetic language. Be aware that while art may form a strong foundation for creative exploration, artworks are protected by copyright legislation. Copying artistic work outright for any commercial use without the express consent of the copyright owner is a crime.

Historical and vintage sources: History provides a treasure trove of creative stimulation. Designers regularly take

inspiration from images of historical and vintage garments, whether from portraiture, photographic documentation, museum garment collections, or thrift stores. Study of period and vintage costume can also be done by observing movies set in the period being explored. In this case, it is best to prioritize movies filmed in the period in question (*Charade*, for example, if researching the style of the early 1960s), or movies known for the historical accuracy of their costumes (perhaps *Vatel* for the late 17th century, or *The King's Speech* for the 1930s). While historical references can provide valuable guidance for experimentation, it must not be forgotten that designing fashion requires a focus on contemporary esthetics. Simply replicating historical styles is likely to generate outcomes that appear "costumy" and lack relevance to a current fashion consumer.

Ethnic and religious sources: Ethnic groups, tribal societies, and religious communities often use items of dress and forms of cultural expression that fall outside the esthetic norms of commercial fashion. This means that fashion designers regularly find such sources intriguing and may choose to take inspiration from, say, an Inuit coat, a

Above: Indigenous cultures are a rich source of creative potential for textiles, shape, color, and much more. However, appropriation of cultural heritage can be a minefield.
Right: Youth cultures, such as neo-punk, create new trends from which designers can benefit.

Papua headdress, or a Masai beading technique. It is essential to remember that many of the clothing styles displayed by these groups stem from spiritual beliefs, so appropriation of them by fashion designers can be problematic. Awareness of the cultural background and spiritual values pertaining to fabrics, garments, accessories, or forms of dress is fundamental and can help to ensure that the ultimate outcome does not cause offense.

Youth culture: Many subcultures have developed unique styles. Punk, goth, grunge, and kawaii, for example, have added to the visual spectrum of style by designing and combining garments in unique ways. Each one of these subcultures evolved out of a specific political and cultural context, often as an expression of anti-establishment beliefs. The visual inspiration that can be drawn from these groups should therefore be considered and understood holistically as a complex social expression, not merely a superficial visual reference.

Fashion research: Researching contemporary fashion for inspiration can be tricky. Most research focused on current fashion can be purposefully used for brand positioning and

competitive analysis (see page 49), as this research primarily informs designers about what is already on the market. Consequently, it is not particularly useful in the development of forward-thinking, innovative designs. When gathering fashion research, designers should favor unique, original ideas, which may come from avant-garde designers or from street style. Researchers must remain aware that replicating another designer's technique or style is unlikely to contribute effectively to creative product development and brand messaging.

Nature and the built environment: Many designers take inspiration from natural forms (such as seashells, waves, flowers, or trees), or the built environment (citing architectural structures such as Gothic cathedrals or the improbable buildings of Frank Gehry). Researching the appearance of objects and places offers potentially interesting material to explore through the design process, and can be a valuable source for textile development, surface experimentations, silhouette play, and much more. By the same token, focusing on object-based research may also at times cause the final product to lack a human touch.

Sketchbook drawing by Gabriel Villena, who was gathering information
and research from direct observation.

Creating Original Research

All the sources and avenues of research listed above are likely to provide designers with existing visual material produced by others. Inevitably, this has its limitations, so the best way to address any "gaps" in available research is to produce new, original research content, known as primary research. There are several techniques for producing original creative research materials, the most common of which are listed below.

Observational drawing: Drawing is a powerful tool, and the process of recording things through drawing can unlock a deeper understanding of the subject matter being documented. In this way, an observational sketch of a vintage garment or an architectural structure can contribute to an enhanced comprehension of the subject's details, surface qualities, proportions, and volumes. All of these elements are often overlooked when glancing quickly at photographic research. Those employing this technique must concentrate on observational documentation, not interpretation. In this context, croquis sketching of vintage garments is not a suitable approach to documentation, as the technique of croquis sketching itself requires the distortion and elongation of the body form, which in turn results in skewed garment proportions.

Photography/video: The digital age has made it possible to record visual information instantly. However, researchers planning to record visual material through photography or videography should use these tools with specific intention. It is far too easy to take a picture that lacks both the clarity and esthetic value required for use in creative design development. If the research is being done for the sake of documentation, the images taken should be fully detailed, including multiple angles and close-up shots, and taken in good lighting to provide a thorough understanding of the subject at hand. If the photos or video are being produced for the development of artistic visual research, the resulting material should meet the qualitative esthetic language of fine-art photography and videography.

Visualization and abstraction: Text-based and other non-visual forms of research are likely to require a process of visualization or abstraction in order to generate research content that can be used through the design-development phase. Employing techniques such as drawing, painting, or collage allows designers to translate poems, lyrics, novels, or even music and other non-visual works of art into inspirational visuals. While some approaches may take on an illustrative direction (for example, showing the visual appearance of what words describe), more abstract methods can produce very exciting creative results. Automatism, gesture art, and action art are some of the techniques that can translate the emotional value of text-based research in ways that transcend logic, and connect more directly and artistically with the viewer.

Intense saturated hues and achromatics alternate in this fashion show
finale, for an appealingly balanced outcome.

Establishing a Color Story

Color selection is an essential step in the research and design processes. Consumers first connect with fashion objects not by focusing on garment construction or design detail, but by perceiving colors instinctively. Careful color selection can make the difference between customers choosing to walk into a store or not. Many consumers have strong, impulsive and, for the most part, subconscious reactions to color that often seem to defy explanation. That said, chromatic selection can be guided by certain core rules of color theory aimed at ensuring a certain level of intentionality and structure in the design outcomes. It is therefore extremely worthwhile to understand some of these key rules of color application in fashion.

Another important consideration is the narrative value of color schemes. Color is essential in communicating the designer's creative inspiration. Similarly, color combinations can communicate messages that may, at times, go against the intentions of the designer. For example, white, aqua, turquoise, and ultramarine will likely remind the viewer of warm seas, while lavender, ecru, dusty blue, and sage may communicate an esthetic connection to Provence and the rural south of France. Consumers, unaware of the intentions of the designer, will probably make the most direct interpretation of the designs being shown, particularly when it comes to color. Designers must therefore always be aware of the way the colors they wish to use are likely to be interpreted by their intended consumers.

Color coding, terminology, and key color schemes

In any industrial environment, coding color consistently ensures that all teams involved in developing and producing a certain product are guided by the same information. Producing a fashion line involves working with dozens of suppliers, vendors, and consultants, often spread across multiple continents. Therefore, specifying color verbally (for example, "spruce green") may lead to misinterpretation along the way. Companies such as Pantone and Coloro have developed standardized color coding systems that allow all companies to communicate accurately. Whenever presenting color in a design process, it is valuable to include Pantone or Coloro coding information for easy referencing.

To apply color effectively, familiarity with the basic terminology and core rules of color theory is required. Refer to the **color wheel** on page 78 to visualize the following terminology.

Hue: A specific mix of primary colors, such as cyan (pure primary), purple (secondary), or yellow–orange (tertiary). Any hue can be the starting point for color development.

Primary colors: These are blue, red, and yellow. These colors can be mixed in order to form all other hues on the color wheel.

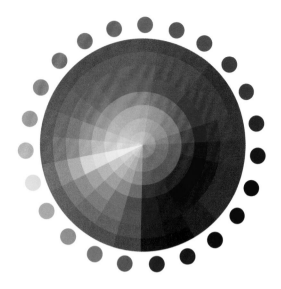

Complementary colors

Analogous colors

Triadic colors

Split complementary
colors

Rectangular double
complementary colors

Square double
complementary colors

The color wheel. The pure hue (indicated in the bubble to the outside of the wheel) is divided into shades and tints.

Secondary colors: The hues achieved by mixing two primary colors together (e.g. green from blue and yellow).

Tertiary colors: The hues achieved by mixing a primary color with a secondary color (e.g. blue–green, or red–purple).

Tint: The various derivative colors resulting from mixing any hue with white. On the color-wheel diagram, tints are closest to the center of the image.

Shade: The various derivative colors resulting from mixing any hue with black. In the diagram, shades are shown in the outer rings of the wheel.

Achromatic colors: White, black, and shades of gray, which contain no hue.

Saturation: The visual intensity or vibrancy of a hue.

Now that we have established basic color terminology, we can move on to define key color schemes. Apart from monochromatic, the following schemes are illustrated above.

Monochromatic: A color scheme composed of only one hue. This may still include the use of tints and shades, or achromatic colors.

Complementary: A two-color scheme composed of hues found in diametric opposition on the color wheel (e.g. red–green, or yellow–purple).

Analogous: A color scheme making use of hues directly adjacent to each other on the color wheel (e.g. blue + blue–purple + purple, or yellow + yellow–green + green).

Triadic: A three-color scheme composed of colors evenly spaced on the color wheel (such as red + blue + yellow, or yellow–orange + red–purple + blue–green).

Split complementary: A three-color scheme formed of a hue from one side of the color wheel plus two hues sitting next to its direct complementary.

Rectangular double complementary: A four-color scheme composed of two sets of complementaries not evenly spaced on the color wheel.

Square double complementary: A four-color scheme composed of two sets of complementaries evenly spaced on the color wheel.

While these standard rules of color combination should be referred to as a foundation for color selection, designers should not forget that – like the instinctive color reactions experienced by their customers – they should use their own creative intuitions and esthetic sensibility when selecting colors. If a color doesn't "feel" right as part of a color selection, that is a powerful indicator that it should be edited out or replaced.

Color palettes and color bars

Color selection should first be established through the development of a **color palette**. The palette is simply a

collection of the relevant color swatches (or color chips) that will be employed in the collection development. Developing color chips by mixing gouache or acrylic paints, collecting interior paint chips from hardware stores, or developing color palettes digitally through Photoshop or Illustrator, can all be suitable starting points. Each of these approaches may, however, present a challenge moving forward: namely, the difficulty the designer may experience in sourcing these specific colors in the current textile marketplace. While relying on the color predictions published by forecasting firms such as WGSN or Peclers can ensure easier sourcing processes, true **innovators** often choose to employ unique hues outside the predicted commercial palettes. This means that achieving those exact colors on fabric will require working with dye labs and printing specialists, who will be tasked to develop custom visual color matches.

In a color palette, all color swatches should be the same size, and swatches should be organized neatly so as to provide an effective reference for print developers, textile producers, and merchandising specialists. Palettes should include all colors that will be employed in the collection,

Above: A color board can help communicate how a chosen color palette connects thematically to visual research. Additionally, a strong color palette can be extracted directly from key images of the research by using Adobe Photoshop, or by visual color matching.

including **seasonal colors** and **staple colors** (neutrals, shades of beige and brown, navy, and achromatics).

A **color bar** uses the colors from the palette in specific arrangements, illustrating the quantitative presence of each color in the proposed range. Color bars are rectangles divided into smaller sections of varying sizes, each filled with a different color from the palette. One palette can generate hundreds of diverse color bars, each of which will express the inspiration and mood of the collection differently. Designers should therefore use this process to visualize a broad variety of possible color combinations in order to make the best-informed decision in the end. The color palette and color bar will act as guidelines for fabric sourcing, textile and design development, and collection **editing**.

| PQ-2459C | PQ-107C | PQ-286C | PQ-2113C | PQ-2067C |
| PQ-CoolGray2C | PQ-426C | PQ-2011C | PQ-118C | PQ-3308C |

A color palette **(above)** and corresponding color bars **(right)**.

Sourcing Materials

Once a designer has established their concept direction for a line, and identified how this concept will expand into a body of research and possible color applications, it is time to source materials. Materials form the basis for all types of design development. Before launching into creative exploration, designers must therefore assemble an ample selection of fabrication options that will support the collection's ideation and realization. Some key considerations must be made while sourcing material options, including purpose, applicability, market context, and useability in a production-based industry.

Diversity, purpose, and price in fabric sourcing

Many successful designers present a wide variety of garment options to their consumers each season. Product diversity is key to ensuring that the collections successfully cater to the needs of buyers and consumers. Anticipating this diversity is therefore a valuable consideration when collecting fabric options. While fall/winter lines will present more outerwear and layered outfits, even spring/summer collections are likely to include a variety of **separates**, jackets, knitwear, outerwear, and suchlike. Effective fabric sourcing should initially consist in gathering a vast selection of options for all sorts of garment uses, which can be edited as the collection takes shape.

Another factor to consider when gathering fabrics is the intended price point of the final product. Fabrics should enhance and support the value of the product within its proposed price bracket. For example, selecting a cheap polyester satin for a range of designer-level evening gowns would be counterproductive, as the consumer would be puzzled by the inferior material in a luxury product. Similarly, using a luxury cashmere in a product directed at a moderate **market level** will make the outcome overpriced and out of reach of its intended consumer.

Sourcing for commercial products

Even the most innovative designers are participating in an industry focused on producing and selling apparel in a commercially minded way. With the exception of **showpieces**, which serve an exclusively narrative function but fall outside commercial considerations, garments must be made of fabrics that can be used for **production runs**. In this way, when a collection is presented to buyers, pieces can be replicated in the quantity required by the **retailer**. This means that obtaining fabrics from local stores is generally not a suitable approach to material sourcing. Local fabric stores might offer some interesting and unexpected options, and serve as an additional source of creative inspiration, but when it comes to developing work for the industry, designers should focus on obtaining fabrics directly from fabric mills (or their agents).

The best way to connect with fabric mills is to plan a sourcing trip to **fabric trade shows**. These are held many times a year, in a multitude of key global locations, and are aimed specifically at connecting **manufacturers** (and designers) with the suppliers they need. As new shows are regularly added to the calendar, a simple online search for fabric trade shows will provide ample information on those taking place in a given geographical region. Designers planning

Above: Fashion manufacturers source fabrics by attending shows such as Première Vision.
Right: Textile trade shows display fabrics for a wide range of purposes.

to attend textile trade shows must also keep in mind that each one is likely to focus on a segment of the marketplace in terms of product pricing.

Many fabric trade shows are scheduled to coincide with the beginning of design processing for a specific season within the traditional fashion calendar. However, if the sourcing effort is being conducted outside this scheduling framework, designers can always reach out to mills directly. Many trade shows publish contact information for their exhibitors and can therefore be a useful resource all year round.

Whether connecting in person during a trade-show event, or off-season by making direct contact with the agents and sales team of the mills, the purpose of sourcing in this way is to collect as many fabric samples as possible, all of which can be ordered in larger quantities if the collection is picked up by buyers. Many mills will also offer the possibility of obtaining **sample yardage**, which will allow a designer to produce the prototypes for the collection without having to

commit to ordering an entire roll of the material. Another key advantage of working directly with fabric mills is that their pricing is usually substantially lower than in fabric stores, as they sell their materials at **wholesale** prices.

Working with textile mills can require a fair amount of pre-planning and additional time in obtaining the required samples, but this will prove a valuable investment for any designer focused on creating commercially viable products.

Above: This line by Colombian brand A New Cross mostly uses staple fabrics, enhancing its trans-seasonal retail potential.

Below: Seasonal prints at a textile trade show.
Bottom: Greige fabrics can be easily dyed or printed.

Staple and seasonal fabrications

Staple fabrications, like staple colors, play an important role in grounding any fashion collection. Staple fabrics are likely to appear regularly, season after season, as they do not follow seasonal trends. Materials such as poplin, twill, serge, **jersey**, crepe, and many others are commonly sourced regardless of the specific collection under development. Many design labels establish a core of staple fabrics, which they usually keep in stock throughout the year.

Seasonal fabrications, as the name suggests, are limited in use to a specific season. They include materials in seasonal colors, fabrics with seasonal prints or surface treatments, and materials woven or knitted specifically to meet that season's trend predictions. While designers can source seasonal materials from fabric trade shows (some trade shows specialize in prints, fabric finishing, embroidery, etc.), many develop their own creative fabrics as part of their design process. Supporting this creative step requires the sourcing of basic materials, called **greige goods**. These fabrics, which include muslin (or **calico**), are usually unfinished, and allow designers to apply their own unique prints, dyeing techniques, embroideries, embellishments, manipulations, or surface treatments onto them.

Water pollution caused by textile dyeing factories in India.

Environmental and ethical considerations in fabric and material sourcing

Materials provide the foundation for all apparel products. The fashion industry is currently under increased scrutiny regarding its ethical and environmental practices, and many of these concerns stem directly from textile processes. It is therefore very important to be aware of the provenance and impact of each material being sourced, particularly those brands aiming to promote themselves as environmentally or socially responsible.

Fiber production and processing are having dire effects on our planet. Even "natural" materials, such as cotton, require extensive use of pesticides and insecticides, which can adversely affect ecosystems and the health of farming communities.

Dyeing of textile products generates alarming amounts of pollutants, which are all too frequently released into public waterways. Leather dyeing in particular demands the use of chemicals scientifically linked to cancer, liver conditions, and nervous system disorders in the communities living close to leather tanneries.

Similarly, some materials – silk, wool, leather, and fur, for example – have been directly linked to animal-welfare concerns.

These are only a few of the current concerns affecting the textile industry. Designers and industry stakeholders are encouraged to research these concerns further by referring to the list of further reading (see pages 218–19).

4. Textile development

Learning objectives

- Understand the valuable role played by creative textiles in the development of a collection

- Identify the structure and the creative applications of constructed surfaces, including woven and knitted fabrications

- Explore the technical context and aesthetic possibilities of dye applications

- Identify a variety of types and creative uses of printed and patterned materials

- Classify embellished surfaces and evaluate their esthetic capabilities

- Evaluate the technical processes and creative applications of manipulated fabrics

- Introduce the technical and esthetic uses of laser-cutting in fashion

- Explore new technologies and fabrication processes impacting the fashion industry

Creative Textile Development

The development and use of original fabrics are essential for designers and **product developers** seeking to strengthen the brand vision expressed in a collection, or to propose truly unique material offerings.

The functional needs of clothing tend to limit the extent to which a designer can push **silhouette** and **construction** while maintaining wearability. This means that fabrics are in many instances the main creative playground for generating interest and value in a product.

Designing a fashion collection demands both in-depth awareness of material processes and the ability to implement them. Smaller fashion companies will likely place textile-design responsibilities within the design or product-development team, which means fashion designers can be expected to develop materials directly or work in close creative collaboration with dedicated textile experts.

This chapter highlights the main avenues of creative textile development employed by design and product-development teams, covering a range of approaches, from the most craft-driven to the most technological. Let's start by establishing some textile terms.

Core textile terminology

Fiber: *The smallest component that makes up textile materials, fiber can come from natural sources (silk, cotton, wool, or linen, for example), or be manufactured (rayon, polyester, and nylon). Fibers that occur or are produced in short segments are referred to as* **staple fibers,** *while fibers harvested or produced as single, long continuous strands are called* **filament fibers.**

Yarn: *A thread usually resulting from spinning (or twisting) fibers together. The finest filament yarns made of synthetic materials may be produced from a single unspun fiber.*

Fabrication: *The process of making cloth by manipulating fibers or yarns. While felting is a form of fiber-based fabrication, weaving and knitting are yarn-based. Some materials, such as vinyl and polyurethane, are achieved by solidifying plastic solutions, which means they are made without the involvement of fibers or yarns.*

Finishing: *Processes applied to fabrics to complete their production and make them market-ready. Finishings can be esthetic, such as printing and* **embossing,** *or functional, such as fireproofing and boiling.*

Opposite: The juxtaposition of original woven, printed, and knitted materials can open unexpected creative possibilities.

Constructed Surfaces

The vast majority of fashion materials, with the exception of pelts and skins such as leather and fur, fit into two main categories of fabric: wovens and knits. These categories refer to the type of **fabrication** process used to transform yarns into usable cloth. Each type of fabrication approach has its own technical properties, as well as unique creative possibilities.

Woven fabrications

As a method of producing fabrics, weaving predates the establishment of the earliest civilizations. In fact, it was first employed to make baskets and other containers out of reeds as far back as the Neolithic period, c.9000 BCE.

Weaving requires the interlacing of two sets of yarns. All the yarns following the lengthwise direction of the finished cloth are called the **warp**, while those going from side to side are referred to as the **weft** (or filling). The process of crisscrossing strands of material together creates a durable, resilient surface that can be used for both draped and tailored garments.

The threads making up the warp and weft grant the woven material stability and strength, which is why most garments made of woven fabrics are constructed by aligning the **grain** (the lengthwise direction of the cloth running parallel to the **selvedge**) with the vertical direction in the finished garment. Garments that require fluidity and softness, on the other hand, can be constructed by cutting the entire garment at a 45-degree angle to the straight grain.

Most woven fabrics fall into one of the following categories.

Plain weave: In this structure the warp and weft cross each time they meet. Plain weaves are commonly used in shirtings and silk fabrics, such as poplin and taffeta.

Oxford: In this plain-weave variation, groups of two or more yarns are manipulated as a single yarn. The final effect resembles a basket-weave surface.

Twill: While each row follows a very simple, regular pattern, twill gains its characteristic diagonal surface quality by shifting the entire structure by a given amount with each new row. Denim, serge, and drill cloths are all types of twill.

Herringbone: This variation of twill gives a zigzag texture to the resulting fabric. It is commonly used in suitings, jacketings, shirtings, and outerwear materials.

Satin: Lengthening the distance between one intersection of warp and weft and the next gives the resulting cloth a glossy surface quality. Usually, this technique requires a second warp to impart enough structure to the fabric to make it usable. This is why many satins are referred to as satin-faced chiffon, satin-faced organza, or crepe-back satin.

Crepe: This term refers to a family of materials with peculiar qualities. Crepes generally have a pebbly surface, a spongy feel, and a bouncy, lively drape. Crepes require very complicated weaving patterns and overtwisted yarns, which impart a springy quality to the final fabrics. Light crepes include georgette and crepe de chine, but crepe can also be made into tailoring-weight cloths.

Complex weaves: Any fabric combining multiple structures from the list above in a single material can be considered a complex weave. Dobby, **jacquard**, and brocade fit into this category, and all present intricate textural effects and patterning.

The weaving process itself can offer many opportunities for creative experimentation, all of which can be explored quite easily by sampling ideas on a small handloom. Any

DIRECTIONS OF A WOVEN CLOTH

STANDARD WOVEN STRUCTURES

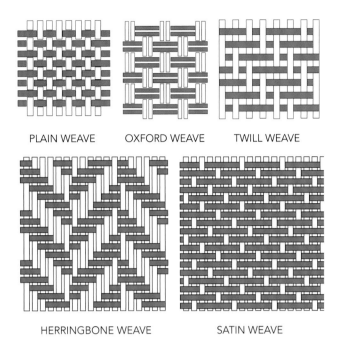

PLAIN WEAVE   OXFORD WEAVE   TWILL WEAVE

HERRINGBONE WEAVE   SATIN WEAVE

idea visualized on a sample loom can then become the starting point for collaboration with a professional weaving mill so that yardage of the fabric can be produced.

Texture

Selecting textured yarns, such as bouclé, or a variety of yarns of different colors and surface qualities, can produce woven **fabrications** with extensive surface interest. A multitude of fashion brands make regular use of unique textural wovens as part of their brand messaging. The house of Chanel is well known for developing custom-designed seasonal variations of tweed, taking the creative capabilities of weaving to a luxurious new level. Designers experimenting with textural wovens should consider the variety of materials available to them, from fluffy angora yarns to metallic Lurex, and from rustic hemp to glossy strips of patent leather. These options must then be evaluated and selected based on the creative and narrative needs of the concept being explored, as well as the functional purpose of the fabrications sampled.

Stripes and checks

The very nature of weaving, structured by the crisscrossing of yarns in two directions, makes it surprisingly easy to create stripes and checks. By simply varying the color of yarns being used in the warp and weft, a designer can create a variety of geometric patterns, from the simple pinstripe to the most intricate tartans.

Most striped and checked woven fabrics in the fashion industry are produced in this way, and not by printing the pattern onto a plain-colored material. This is because weaving stripes from dyed yarn will ensure better longevity of the final material. These are usually referred to in design-development processes as **yarn-dyed fabrics**.

From rustic tattersall and gingham to dressed-up chalkstripe, and from traditional houndstooth to fun and futuristic optic stripes, the creative possibilities are endless.

When it comes to designing a stripe or check pattern, the best first step is to visualize the design through the use of traditional drawing and artistic media. Once an initial design direction has been established, making use of specialized weaving digital software can be much faster than experimenting by hand, particularly as so many of these striped and checked fabrics are realized in very fine yarns. Basic familiarity with programs such as Pointcarré Dobby or Textronic Design Dobby can be of great value when communicating design ideas to fabric mills.

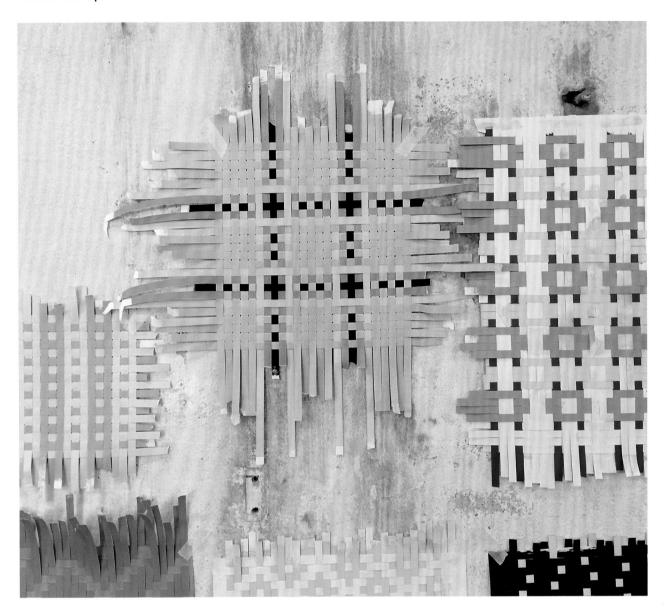

Cultural identity and tartan

Tartan patterns have a long history and play a distinctive and meaningful part within Celtic culture. Individual tartan patterns indicate affiliation to a specific clan or family, so they are worn proudly, as a sign of identity and honor.

Designers making use of tartan fabrics should be keenly aware of this cultural context, and respect its historical value. Working directly with a Scottish or Irish mill toward the development of a proprietary tartan for a fashion brand can be a way to pay homage to this rich and fascinating heritage.

Complex wovens

Dobby, jacquards, and brocades make use of multiple weaving structures to achieve inticate surface texture and patterning. These materials are usually fabricated using fine yarns, such as silks and cottons, in the creation of light- to midweight materials for **apparel** use. Due to the intricate construction of these fabrics, experimenting with them by hand-sampling is incredibly difficult. Designs proposed for a jacquard or brocade should first be designed by hand or computer (just like print designs, see page 100), and then translated into weaving patterns by using dedicated weaving design software, as mentioned above.

Opposite: Creative weaving experiments: *We Salute the Sketch*
by textile designers Helle Gråbæk and Maria Kirk Mikkelsen.
Below: Mixing jacquards, prints, and embroidery is a core creative
signature of Belgian designer Dries van Noten.

Complex weaving explained

*Many fashion-industry professionals use the terms dobby,
jacquard, brocade, and damask in possibly confusing
ways. Each term, though, does have a specific meaning
and should therefore be used accurately.*

Dobby: *The surface of dobby fabrics presents small,
simple, geometric textural patterns, such as stripes,
diamonds, or dots. Dobby fabrics are most commonly
used for shirting-weight construction. The term
"dobby" is also used by textile designers to refer to a
specific type of weaving machinery used in the production
of this fabric.*

Jacquard: *A multicolored woven fabric, presenting
intricate patterns, such as florals. Some jacquards are
finished on both sides, while others may have long strands
of unwoven yarn called "floats" on the back, in which case
their usability will be limited to lined garments and ties.
The term "jacquard" is also used by weavers to refer to
a specific type of computerized loom system used in the
production of many complex wovens.*

Brocade: *A multicolored complex weave with intricate
patterning and texture. Brocade usually refers to heavy
fabrics used for outerwear or accessories. The name derives
from the Italian broccato, meaning "embossed cloth."*

Damask: *A mid- to heavyweight textural woven fabric
finished on both sides, and commonly used in jackets,
coats, and accessories. Damasks traditionally use only two
colors, although some variations have been produced to
achieve polychromatic results. Damask originated in the
city of Damascus, in present-day Syria.*

WEFT KNIT

WARP KNIT

Knitted fabrications

Instead of crisscrossing warp and weft, as in weaving, knitted fabrics are created by looping a yarn around itself or other looping yarns. This allows the production of cloths with two distinct properties that set them apart from wovens: insulation and stretch.

Within the knitted family, there are two overarching groups of materials, **warp knits** and **weft knits**. In warp knits, yarns go predominantly in a vertical direction in the finished cloth. The various materials belonging to this category include tricot, knit piqué, raschel, and Milanese, often found in specialist markets such as activewear and lingerie. Due to the complexity of warp knits, they tend to be produced mainly by machine rather than hand.

By contrast, weft knits see the yarns going predominantly side to side. They are constructed by arranging knit stitches and **purl** stitches in a particular order, most often creating clean vertical alignments called **wales**. **Jersey**, waffle knit, rib, cable, and **Fair Isle**, among many others, are all weft knits.

Opposite: This look by Johan Ku, makes use of experimental knitting techniques.

While warp knits are notoriously challenging to produce by hand, weft knits in heavier yarns (sweater-weight and up) can easily be sampled through hand techniques, involving the creative arrangement of simple stitches.

Knitted garments are divided into two types: **cut-and-sew knits** and **fashioned knits**. Cut-and-sew construction is achieved by using yardage of fine knitted fabrics such as jersey, knit fleece, or piqué, cutting out garment pieces, then assembling them using **serging machines**. This allows the production of cheaper garments in less time, but does generate a fair bit of waste.

Fashioned knits, on the other hand, make use of the specific capabilities of knitting, particularly a technique called a "decrease," to create shaped garment pieces directly from yarn. The edges of these pieces are then linked together to form the finished garment. This technique is more likely to be used in sweater-weight production, and is somewhat more costly than cut-and-sew. However, it does virtually eliminate material waste in the production process.

While materials used in cut-and-sew construction are usually referred to by weight (measured in ounces per square yard, or grams per square meter), sweater-weight knits are most likely to be described by **gauge**. This term

refers to the number of stitches present in 1 inch (2.5 cm) of a weft knit measured horizontally along the knitted row. Therefore, a 12-gauge knit will be finer than a 4-gauge knit. Most commonly, the size of the yarn being used is planned in accordance with the intended gauge of the material under development.

Weft knits provide extensive opportunities for creativity and experimentation, whether this is sampled by hand, or by using relatively user-friendly knitting machinery. While some of the techniques listed below are focused on color play, others are driven primarily by adding texture and surface interest.

Stripes
Since weft knits are constructed in successive rows, it is really easy to produce them in stripes. Simply varying the color of the yarn being used for any row can add visual interest to the material. Like woven stripes, knitted stripes can vary from the simple Breton stripe to the most complex graphic patterning. Very subtle stripes can be produced by playing with yarns that differ mostly in sheen or texture rather than color.

Intarsia
One way to create more complex multicolor knits is to use a technique called intarsia. This requires the introduction of a different colored yarn for a specific section of the knitted fabric. In this case, the yarns are worked in such a way as to produce a single-layer fabric showcasing areas of color. Any pattern can be a starting point for intarsia work, from florals to geometrics. Argyle knits, which originated in Scotland, are a specific variation of the intarsia technique.

Fair Isle and double knits
It is possible to create pretty complex variations of weft knits by running two yarns (rather than one) in any given row. This allows the knitter to choose which yarn, and therefore which color, to use for the right side of the cloth at any given time, and this in turn enables the creation of intricate patterns. Fair Isle knits show the unused yarn running horizontally on the reverse of the material, while double knits produce a finished knitted surface on both sides.

Opposite left: The bee in this Lindy Bop sweater is achieved using the intarsia knitting technique.

Opposite right: A Fair Isle sweater on the runway at the Michael Kors Fall 2018 show.

Designing for intarsia, Fair Isle, and double knits

*Patterns for these techniques can very easily be visualized on paper or a computer screen. This step can provide opportunities for the **ideation** of numerous design options before committing more substantial time to making knitted samples.*

Designers should begin by compiling an inventory of all the colors they will be able to use, by sourcing samples of the colors available in their chosen yarn.

Visualizing knitted patterns requires the use of a gauge graph, a simple template that indicates the actual size of each individual stitch in the finished knitted fabric. Each stitch can then be colored in by hand or on screen to provide a preview of how the actual material will look.

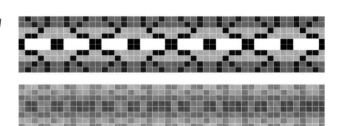

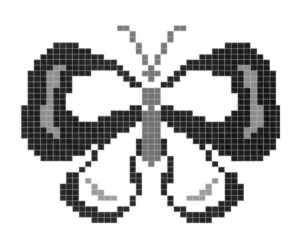

Fair Isle **(above right)** and intarsia designs **(right)** visualized using a gauge graph.

Simple textural knits
By varying the order of the knit and purl stitches, it is possible to create more interesting surfaces, which will appear to dip or protrude in given areas. This category includes rib knits, in which groups of knit stitches and purl stitches are placed in the same regular order in each row, as well as more complex waffle knits, checkerboard knits, or chevrons, which require more complex placements of stitches to achieve the required outcome.

Cables and knit lace
While the basic knitting techniques are very easy to master, there are more challenging ones that can produce complex visual results. Most simple knits place stitches in wales, but it is possible to take groups of stitches and move them sideways with each new row. This creates a diagonal or wave-like textural change, and is at the core of a large group of knitted fabrics called **cable knits**.

It is also possible to take a single stitch and split it into two while creating the next row. This creates a visible hole in the material, which can be used intentionally as a decorative element, as in knit lace.

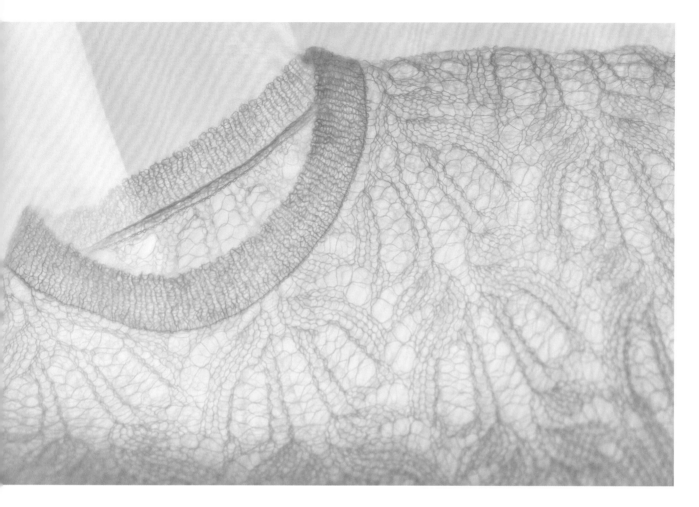

Lightweight cable-knit sweater by Delpozo.

Non-traditional fabrications

Many designers creating products for the more creative segments of the fashion market have been challenging traditional processes of fabrication. Through research into less common forms of fabrication, these designers have redefined the boundaries between craft and industrial manufacturing, or ventured into high-tech new arenas.

Techniques such as felting, macramé, braiding, crochet, bobbin lacemaking, and many others traditionally designated as craft applications have provided a fertile ground for rediscovery and reinvention of material construction for fashion.

Similarly, innovative technologies for weaving, knitting, and braiding have allowed the development of new types of fashion product, such as 3D-knitted running shoes and seamless woven clothing items. This type of technological rethinking of fabrication processes is most effectively accomplished by collaborating closely with industrial engineers who are developing the machinery. Indeed, it makes this new way of ideating fashion product possible.

Dye Applications

Another arena for the creative exploration of textiles as part of a collection-development process resides in dye-based techniques. Of course, many materials sourced earlier in the collection research already present specific colors, but dyeing techniques can offer so much more.

Dyeing is a chemical process in which molecules of dye become chemically attached to a fiber. Different fibers require different types of dye in order for this chemical reaction to take place correctly, and these are outlined below.

DYE TYPES AND INTENDED FIBERS		
Type of dye	Suitable fibers	Technical requirements
Direct dyes (a.k.a. Substantive dyes)	Cellulosic fibers, such as cotton, linen, nettle, rayon.	High water temperature and salt.
Acid dyes	Protein fibers, including silk and wool.	High water temperature and acetic acid (vinegar).
Basic dyes	Acrylic.	High water temperature and acetic acid.
Reactive dyes	Silk and cellulosic fibers, such as cotton.	Most reactive dyes work effectively with cold water and salt.
Disperse dyes	Primarily used for synthetic fibers, including polyester, nylon, and acrylic.	Some disperse dyes require a pressurized dye vat to achieve the necessary dye temperature of 266°F (130°C).
Mordant dyes	Suitable for a broad variety of materials, dependent on the specific combination of dye and **mordant** selected.	These dyes are notoriously complex and diverse. Natural dyes are part of this category, as are chrome dyes, commonly used to dye wool and leather. Some of these require the use of environmentally problematic chemicals.
Vat dyes	Cellulosic and protein fibers.	Vat dyes, including natural indigo, need to be chemically dissolved in order to be applied to fibers. Exposure to oxygen in the drying process then causes the dye to retake its intended color.
Azoic dyes, sulfur dyes, and other developed dyes	Suitable for a variety of materials, depending on the specific type of dye being used.	These dyes require the combination of two or more chemicals on the fiber for the creation of the dye molecule. These can generate a highly colorfast result, but require environmentally problematic chemicals.

Another important consideration to note is that fiber dyeing is one of the worst contributors to environmental pollution and toxic chemical runoffs. It commonly requires extensive amounts of water, energy, and noxious chemicals. Understanding these concerns is essential for any brand focused on environmentally responsible sourcing and production. Research into less environmentally damaging dyeing and printing techniques has been fostered over the last few years by companies and trade organizations, such as Colorep and Cotton Incorporated.

Creative dye techniques

Dyeing offers a vast range of creative possibilities for designers and product developers, from the most simple color applications to highly complex artistic expressions. Applying color to textile materials can happen at any stage of development, offering opportunities for extensive creative play. Dyeing fibers prior to spinning is used to generate multicolored or heathered yarns. Dyeing yarns prior to fabrication forms the basis for useful yarn-dyed stripes and checks, while applying dye to woven or knitted fabric allows a solid, shaded, or painterly surface appearance to be created. The main techniques employed in applying dye to yarns and fabrics are outlined below.

Vat-dyeing
Dyeing yarn or fabric by using a dye bath (such as a cooking pot or an industrial dyeing tub) is referred to as vat-dyeing. This technique is used primarily to achieve solid-color applications, but can also be explored creatively. The process of vat-dyeing is the traditional

way of developing custom color matches, so designers looking to use colors not readily available in the marketplace will need to explore the creative capabilities of color mixing in **vat-dyeing**. Mixing dyes to achieve specific color outcomes can take both technical know-how and expertise, but can be a very valuable tool in establishing brand-specific colorways.

Dip-dyeing
Many forms of dyeing focus on partially applying dyes to yarns or fabrics. One such process is **dip-dyeing**, a technique that relies on repeatedly dipping material sections in the dyebath to achieve a color gradient rather than a uniform solid color. The most traditional products of dip-dyeing are commonly called **ombré** (shaded) fabrics. It is also possible to use dip-dyeing techniques to explore more painterly and creatively playful outcomes.

Resist-dyeing
Applying wax, rice paste, or resin onto fabric can prevent it from absorbing dyes in specific areas. This practice forms the basis of a group of textile processes called **resist-dyeing** or **wax-dyeing**. Because of the ease with which it can create complex designs with relatively simple tools, it has been adopted by many different cultures. The best-known fabrics belonging to this family are Indonesian batik, Japanese tsutsugaki, and Yoruba cloth from Nigeria.

The term "resist-dyeing" is sometimes used generically to encompass all dyeing techniques in which dye is stopped from entering the fiber. It actually includes variations of the techniques listed above, and processes of pressure-based prevention, known as **tie-dyeing**.

Above: Shibori, a traditional tie-dyeing technique.
Right: Dye-painted look by Antoni and Alison.

Tie-dyeing

By applying pressure on certain areas of the cloth being dyed, it is possible to prevent those sections from absorbing dye. This technique can be achieved by tying or knotting the fabric, or by using various tools, such as clamps, elastic bands, string, and wooden boards. A specific category of tie-dyeing, originating in 8th-century Japan, is called **shibori** and has been used extensively in fashion products.

Fabric-painting

Just as ink is used for painting on paper, so dyes can be painted directly onto cloth. However, some technical challenges may arise in this process. One difficulty is that most cloths are highly absorbent, causing dye to "run." This can be remedied by applying small areas of synthetic resist to the fabric, which will stop wet dye from seeping across the cloth uncontrolled. Another technical requirement of dyeing, dictated by the type of dye being used, is the need for heat to be applied so that the dyeing reaction can occur. This can be accomplished by steaming or baking cloth after it has been painted at room temperature. Another option to consider would be to paint with reactive dyes, which do not require high heat.

A special technique called ikat requires painting the warp threads before the woven cloth is constructed. This generates a highly recognizable blurriness to the design in the finished material.

Prints and Patterns

The development of printing techniques has made the production of multicolored patterned materials faster, easier, and cheaper than ever before. The three main types of printing techniques present in the fashion marketplace today are screen printing, woodblock printing, and digital printing.

Woodblock printing requires a design pattern to be carved into a piece of wood, which can then be used as a stamp to apply color onto cloth. This technique is very ancient, yet still used today for the production of fabrics such as chintz and paisley.

Screen printing is believed to have originated in China around the beginning of the first millennium CE. Since then, the technique has evolved surprisingly little. Certainly, it has been mechanized and enhanced to allow large quantities of material to be produced, but the core principle is unchanged. Screen printing relies on selective application of dye or pigment using a stencil, which is supported by a mesh screen from which the technique takes its name. Each screen used in producing the design usually prints only one color; the final printed pattern is achieved by careful placement of areas of flat color, leading to what is commonly referred to as a **graphic print**. A big advantage of screen printing is that the screen can be used to apply a variety of pastes to the fabric. This allows the printing of opaque pigment colors, glues used for flocking and foiling, or acid paste used for **burnout** (dévoré).

Digital printing uses advanced mechanical devices, originally developed for office and commercial printing, to print an image directly from a computer screen onto fabric. The ease of this process makes it a particularly valuable tool when exploring the creative potential of **photographic print** designs. The limitations of digital printing rest in two factors: color quality and cost. Due to the way ink is sprayed onto the surface of the cloth by the digital printer, it can be prone to fading and also tricky to color-match. Digital printing is much slower and therefore substantially more expensive than screen printing, particularly when producing a large yardage of a printed fabric.

Above: Block printing, digital printing, and embellishments come together in this look by Boryana Petrova.
Opposite: Mary Katrantzou makes extensive use of digital printing throughout her Fall/Winter 2018 collection.

Developing a print design

The first steps in developing a print design are to determine whether it will be graphic or photographic, how it will make use of the creative research put together for the concept direction of the collection, and whether it will be a placement print, all-over repeat pattern, or engineered print design. Each of these options provides both creative opportunities and challenges, which must be managed through the design process.

Placement prints are designs positioned on a specific area of the fabric or garment. Graphic T-shirts are a good example of how broadly this type of print has been used in certain segments of the industry, for two primary reasons: its ease of production and its visual impact. Brands at the higher end of the marketplace, who are pushing to expand their appeal toward a younger audience, have often made use of placement prints to do so.

Developing a placement print is quite simple. In many ways, whatever can be drawn or designed on paper can easily be applied to cloth, either through a screen-printing or digital-printing process. Designers should be aware that the positioning of placement prints should be determined in such as way that the design does not intersect **seams** or **darts**, as these constructed areas cause difficulties in the printing process.

Allover repeat prints are applied to fabric to cover the entire cloth prior to garment cutting and construction. From mass-market dresses at H&M to couture blouses at Viktor & Rolf, allover prints play an important role in the fashion industry.

Designing an allover repeating print can be challenging at first, but with a little care and patience, it is a process that can be mastered relatively quickly. It is one of those skills that will keep bearing dividends, so it is definitely worth the initial investment of time.

The repeat of a pattern is usually based on a primary design unit, which replicates side to side and top to bottom. The larger the design, the larger this unit is likely to be. This central structure can be repeated by following a standard square pattern, a horizontal subway pattern, called a "brick repeat," or a vertical subway pattern, referred to as a "half-drop." Units can also be designed

Both the shirt and the suit in this Issey Miyake look make use of allover prints. China Fashion Week, 2014.

to reflect vertically or horizontally each time they repeat. Working out the primary design unit can be done by hand, digitally, or through a combination of both. Designers should start by deciding which type of repeat they will work with, then position all of the necessary design elements within the basic unit, being careful to match those elements sitting on the edges of the design. With the exception of simple geometrics, the more complex the design, the more likely it is that the viewer will be unable to easily identify the primary design unit, which generally indicates a more fashion-driven print.

The main purpose of a repeat print design is to create a seamlessly fluid visual impression on the cloth, so a good repeat pattern should appear uniform and complete.

Engineered prints are envisioned as fully three-dimensional patterns that cover the finished garment so that they match exactly on all seams, darts, and closures. This is the most advanced form of print design and requires a thorough understanding of both print development and garment construction.

The development of an engineered print starts with a sketch determining how the garment will look from all angles. Next, the design team has to work out the exact three-dimensional shape of the garment by developing a production-ready **muslin prototype** (toile), while the print design team will be charged with refining and finalizing the various elements that will form the final print.

Once the muslin prototype and the print elements are resolved, the design can be worked out by tracing, drawing, or attaching all the design elements directly onto the muslin prototype. Then the prototype is taken apart by cutting all its seams open after the print has been positioned, which returns the design to a printable 2D format, in the shapes of separate garment pieces. These will be digitized, cleaned up, and organized into a single printable **layout**, which can then be printed onto the final cloth.

One technical issue that has to be considered carefully in the case of engineered prints is the fact that many printing processes can cause fabric to shrink. This has to be tested for and either prevented, by using pre-shrunk fabric, or reverse-engineered into the design process.

An engineered print on show at Dior Haute Couture, Spring 2008.

Specialized digital software such as the Gerber platform has considerably enhanced the ease with which this process can be implemented, but it may not be easily accessible to smaller design teams, so gaining proficiency in creating engineered designs manually can be highly valuable.

Embellishment

The fashion industry makes ample use of embellished surfaces at almost all levels of the marketplace. Embellishing means to sew or attach thread, beads, sequins, or pieces of fabric onto a base material, and hundreds of different techniques exist within this broad family.

Embellishment is as old as civilization. Ancient cultures would adorn cloth with **embroidery** and **beading** to beautify their apparel, as well as to symbolize affluence and therefore social influence. The time-consuming nature of many of these techniques, particularly until the advent of mechanized embroidery, makes the use of embellishment an obvious display of wealth.

Many civilizations have employed embellishments in the development of culturally significant items of dress, from central Asian chainstitch patterns to English **crewelwork**, Samburu beading in Africa, and the ritual robes of Native American medicine men. In-depth research into the cultural meaning of these types of textile design must be carried out by contemporary designers so as not to run the risk of appropriating a culture's traditions disrespectfully.

When producing large amounts of embellished materials, designers can opt for mechanized embellishments, or choose to work with hand-embroidery suppliers. While a few hand embroiderers still operate in Europe, many of these companies nowadays are based in southern Asia, where there is a cultural tradition of embellished fabrications, and inexpensive labor is available.

Manual embellishment in specialized studios generally involves using a **tambour** (from the French, meaning "drum"), a cumbersome frame that supports a large section of fabric and requires the worker to use a specialized tambour hook. This can produce faster results when compared to straight needle embellishment, but does require specialized training. Designers should consider the creative potential of embellishment, and start by making sample surfaces using simple straight-needle techniques. These samples can later be translated into a mechanized or tambour embellishment when moving from creative development to production.

Embellished detail by Delpozo.

Embroidery

Embroidery can be simply defined as the decorative use of sewing techniques. All that is needed is fabric, needle, and thread. While the thickness of the thread (or floss) being used depends on the individual design under development, the basic embroidery stitches applied to fashion products are individually very easy to master.

The topstitched designs on the back pockets of denim jeans are one example of simple yet effective use of embroidery. By using basic stitches creatively, whether by hand or machine, it is possible to generate incredibly complex and luxurious surfaces. The choice of base material and the density of the embroidery work should be made with a clear sense of the ultimate purpose and use of the fabric.

COMMON STITCHES USED IN HAND EMBROIDERY

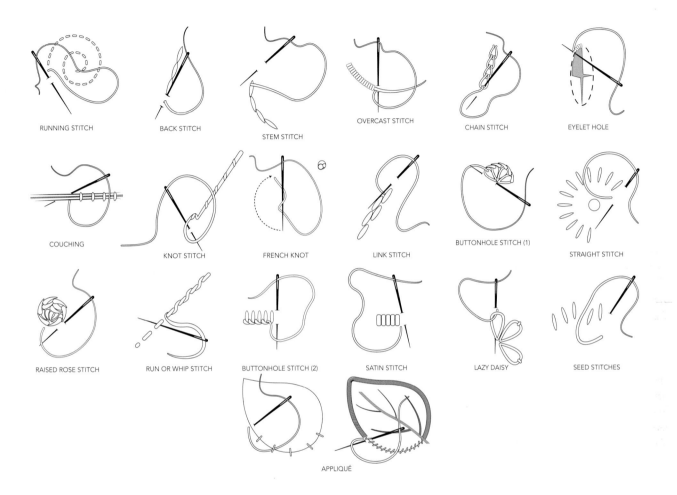

RUNNING STITCH · BACK STITCH · STEM STITCH · OVERCAST STITCH · CHAIN STITCH · EYELET HOLE

COUCHING · KNOT STITCH · FRENCH KNOT · LINK STITCH · BUTTONHOLE STITCH (1) · STRAIGHT STITCH

RAISED ROSE STITCH · RUN OR WHIP STITCH · BUTTONHOLE STITCH (2) · SATIN STITCH · LAZY DAISY · SEED STITCHES

APPLIQUÉ

The same stitches used in embellishing Dior *haute couture* are also commonly used in mass-market childrenswear and craft textile work. Careful qualitative awareness of how the technique is being applied is therefore paramount in ensuring the commercial value of the finished item.

Beading

Beading uses sewing techniques to attach small pieces of glass, crystal, or precious and semi-precious stones onto cloth. Depending on the type of design and materials involved, beading has been traditionally connected with European aristocratic dress, Hollywood glamor, and ethnic attire, and is still predominantly used today within these core narrative contexts.

As the beads themselves are solid and quite dense, beading needs to be carefully planned. Bead placements should be arranged so that they do not interfere with seams or darts, as it is impossible to sew through a densely beaded fabric. The type and quantity of beads used should be carefully decided bearing in mind their weight and the intended function and wearability of the finished product.

Sequin work

While disc-shaped beads have long been used in a variety of traditional embellishment styles, sequin work became an increasingly popular fashion from the late 19th century through to the 1940s. This period marked an increasing focus on commercializing fashion for the middle classes, so presented the perfect opportunity for more inexpensive ways of achieving glitzy shine.

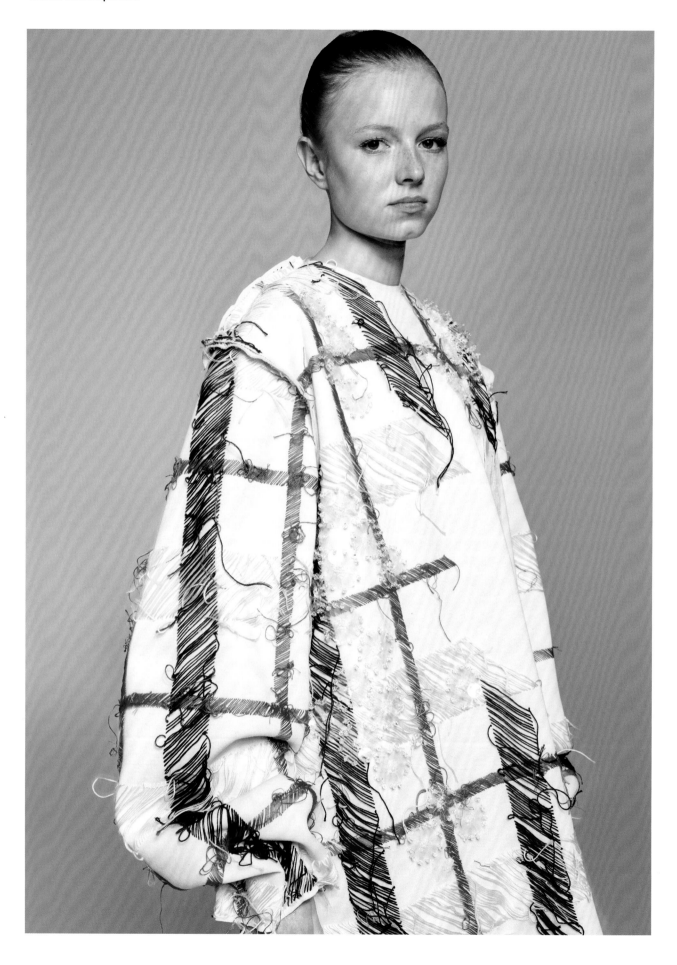

Above left: Playful surface work with sequins, beads, and embroidery by Jessica Grady.
Above center: Delpozo employs sequins to impart shape to draped elements of the garment, combining embellishment and structure.
Right: Bold appliqués at Schiaparelli Haute Couture, Fall 2016.
Opposite: Creative embroidered look by Jodie Ruffle.

Sequins are cheaper, lighter, and faster to attach than beads. While the most complex variations are still executed mostly by hand, it is possible to mechanize the production of simpler sequin materials, making them extremely cost-effective.

Appliqué

Sometimes referred to as "patching," appliqué involves sewing a section of fabric onto a base material using embroidery techniques. Depending on the complexity of the appliqué method used, and on the finesse with which embroidery stitches are employed, the resulting material can vary quite extensively, from rugged military-inspired outerwear to couture-level floral patterns. High-end lace work is commonly executed using appliqué techniques so that the final garment can achieve a seamless look.

Many consumers tend to associate traditional appliqué with childrenswear, as it is often incorporated into this market segment. Designers and product developers should be aware of this connection when developing fashion items intended for adult consumers if they want to avoid the product line appearing overly juvenile.

Glued embellishments

Some items used for embellishment are difficult to sew using standard sewing methods, so they are attached to fabric with special textile glue or heat-sensitive resin. Among these are flatback crystals or rhinestones. The back of these decorative gems is coated with resin, which melts through heat pressing and bonds the crystal to the fabric without any need for sewing. Featherwork is also commonly executed using textile glue.

All the techniques listed above are very often combined for the development of more complex surface designs. Therefore, while developing technical know-how in each group separately can be useful, becoming fluent in all the various tools of embellishment will greatly enhance the interest of the materials a designer may incorporate into their work.

Manipulations

While embellishments are aimed at decorating a base fabric, manipulations tend to focus on changing a material's textural appearance. This can be achieved by various techniques, which are categorized below. The groupings are determined by which technical process is employed to cause the required change in surface quality.

Sewn manipulations
Techniques in this category include **smocking**, **tucking**, **ruching** (gathering or shirring), **patchwork**, **quilting**, and **trapunto**.

All these techniques are achieved by sewing fabric either to itself, or onto another layer, in order to create a controlled three-dimensional surface. The resulting materials can be used in a broad variety of garment types, from sheer summer blouses to protective outerwear.

Heat-set manipulations
Techniques in this category include pleating, **crushing**, and embossing. Many fabrics can be shaped with the careful application of heat and pressure. This can lead to very controlled outcomes, such as pleated materials, or more organic results, such as those generated by crushing. While most natural fibers will lose pleats over time, materials that contain thermoplastic fibers can be pleated or crushed permanently to achieve wash-resistant results.

Embossing is a little more complex, as it requires the use of a metal plate or roller carved into the required design. This technique can be used to create very diverse surfaces, from traditional damask motifs to futuristic geometrics. In leather production, embossing techniques are commonly used to create exotic-looking leathers, such as imitation python or faux alligator.

Surface treatments
Techniques in this category include **brushing**, **sandblasting**, and **stonewashing**. Many brands want their garments to appear worn-in or distressed, as this can provide a sense of

esthetic authenticity to the product, particularly in certain markets such as denim. The process of intentionally aging materials and garments relies on careful execution of a combination of surface treatments. These can be done to fabric before garment cutting and assembly, or applied to garments after construction.

Perforation
As the term suggests, perforation involves cutting holes into fabric. In industry, and particularly when producing large amounts of a perforated fabric, this tends to be done through the use of a cutting die (think of it as a cookie cutter). In order for the perforations to be self-sealed and resistant to fraying, the die plate can be heated up so as to singe the cut edges.

Above: Illustration of a quilted look by Constance Blackaller.
Opposite: Japanese brand FDMTL has built a cult reputation for their washed-denim patchworked coveralls.

Laser-cutting

Laser-cutting, a relatively modern technology that has gained value and relevance in the fashion industry, was made possible by the harnessing of laser light in the 1960s. Industrial lasers can be used to burn into or cut through virtually any material. As soon as this technology became reasonably affordable, fashion designers started employing it for a multitude of creative applications.

Laser-cutting can, of course, be used to cut fully through a material, resulting in a perforated surface, or it can be used to raster (etch) a design onto the surface of the cloth. For example, etching a brocade pattern into satin will cause the burnt areas to be duller than the original satin, giving an embossed look to the finished cloth. Laser-rastering is also commonly used as a finishing process on denim jeans to achieve an aged look in the final garment.

Laser technology offers some major advantages compared to traditional embossing, perforation, or surface treatments – namely its speed, ease of setup, and ability to be used for short product runs without major additional costs.

Most laser-cutting machines set up for fashion materials have very clear and quite user-friendly technical requirements. They are generally compatible with most vector-based graphic-design software (such as Adobe Illustrator). Sampling a laser-cut design is not particularly difficult once access to the machinery is secured. In order to avoid wasted time or unnecessary sampling expenses when working with external suppliers, designers should plan and test their design first. The primary step is to visualize the cutout design by drawing it out, whether by hand or on computer, in simple line work. It is then very useful to print the design onto paper and actually cut it out using a precision knife. This can show up pattern flaws that the designer can correct before progressing to sampling on fabric. Once the pattern has been tested, it can be finalized through a vector-based design software and sent, along with the required fabric, to the laser-cutting specialist.

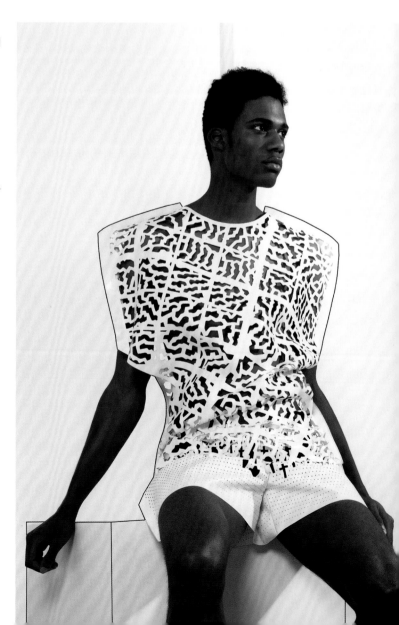

New Technology and Fabrication Development

Many designers focus their creative practice on experimenting with innovative material processes beyond those traditionally associated with garment production. Forward-thinking designers, such as Iris van Herpen, have focused particularly on the use of solution-based materials and **3D printing** technology. Both can offer unique creative applications, redefining how garments are thought up, designed, and constructed.

Working with resins, latex, and other solution-based materials has challenged the traditional boundaries of fabrication, which is normally limited to the production of flat lengths of cloth. The solutions can be molded into three-dimensional forms and take that shape through the curing stages, thus reducing the need for traditional garment shaping and assembling processes.

Similarly, 3D printing (a rapid-prototyping technique) involves the use of advanced machinery to create complex three-dimensional shapes out of thermoplastic materials. While the technical limitations of current 3D printing do not allow for its use in large-scale garment production, the technology is undergoing rapid evolution. While Iris van Herpen, threeASFOUR, and others have been exploring the creative possibilities of 3D printing mainly in the context of showpieces and concept prototypes, many creative leaders consider 3D printing as a likely direction for the fashion industry to consider as it strives to develop more environmentally and socially responsible ways of producing apparel.

Right: Dutch designer Iris van Herpen has built a strong brand vision by exploring the technological boundaries of materials, as in this 3D-printed dress.
Opposite: Laser-cut look by Martijn van Strien.

Designer Profile: Holly Fulton

Holly Fulton is the creative director of her eponymous label.

Your work makes use of a variety of textile techniques. Which ones do you prefer using and why?

My primary love is creating pattern and then rendering it in 3D through a variety of media. Print has always been the core of what we do, but I have always used a lot of plastics. I love the pure shot of color you get with it, and the synthetic vibrancy relates to my love of Pop art and high-shine surfaces. I like to work with materials that can be laser-cut, alongside those such as wood and shell laminates, and mix them with metals, both in bespoke cut form and as studs and more industrial components. My early work utilized a lot of unconventional materials, focused around hardware, and the high–low juxtaposition of these with crystal still excites me.

Tell us about what made you want to be a designer.

I always had a keen interest in fashion but it wasn't until I'd done my foundation course and dabbled with fashion and textiles that I felt it was my vocation. I did an MA at the Royal College of Art [London], and that crystallized my love of design; it allowed my interdisciplinary way of working to flourish, and clothing turned out to be the perfect vehicle for my graphic multimedia style.

How would you describe your brand?

We are a high-end womenswear label with a focus on signature graphics and pattern alongside luxurious fabrications. We create a total look from jewelry, bags, and sunglasses to clothing and footwear. We are known for our use of graphic line and bold color and our primary USP is the fact that all our pattern and embellishment is hand-rendered. I work directly onto the garment patterns to engineer every line, and it is very important to me to understand exactly where each element will sit on the wearer.

What are the main challenges you have encountered while developing your business?

How to balance creativity with business. It is crucial that you have a solid understanding of this in order to support, sustain, and grow your creative vision and team. Balancing the demands of running a label can be challenging; it is an all-consuming job and your dedication can be tested on occasion. It is important to learn to manage other people's expectations as well as your own. Financial pressure, business planning, and an awareness of cashflow to enable you to plan strategically have been sharp learning curves. I have learned to dedicate as much time and energy to strategy as to design.

Why did you choose your specific niche? What opportunities has it provided you?

I think the niche chose me; I was lucky to occupy a space that not many designers do. My way of working, which encompasses the hand-drawn creation of the textile and embellishment while evolving the final look, has allowed me to stand slightly apart. I had not foreseen the opportunity for collaboration; having a signature that is deeply rooted in our graphics and pattern has allowed us to work not just as fashion designers but more broadly as designers across a wide range of product categories with numerous brands. This extension into the broader world of design has been a very positive and exciting adjunct to our original business.

How do you see the future of your segment of the industry?

The fashion landscape is constantly evolving and the established traditions of the industry are shifting. I hope that designers will take sustainability seriously as part of their practice and consider not just the impact of their work but also the message the industry as a whole is projecting. I believe there will always be a place for high-end fashion, but I feel a duty of care to my consumers, and to the example I set within design, to consider my manufacturing and methodology carefully. The digital age has allowed the underdog the opportunity to create a valid business model without taking part in fashion weeks at all. This creative frisson is exciting; new raw talent is given a chance to shine, particularly in London, and I hope that this continues to flourish with a more mindful and environmental approach.

How do your chosen customer and market influence your design approach?

It is fundamental to consider your consumer and the territories that respond best to your work. Through showrooms, trunk shows, **retailer** feedback, and private-client work, we have been able to establish a profile of our customer and design our commercial ranges with her in mind. Our style has not been altered by our client, but enhanced by the idea of her lifestyle and preferences. We want to create pieces that keep her love of our work fresh while also pushing us as designers and challenging contemporary design. We would always consider factors such as climate for our regional stockists, and often work on exclusive ranges for areas that are more season-specific.

5. Design development

Learning objectives

- Explore the many design processes used in creating a collection

- Understand the creative uses of sketching, collage, and digital media in collection development

- Explore a variety of fashion silhouettes

- Identify the multiple approaches and uses of draping on the form

- Find out about digital draping techniques in collection development

- Discover detail-focused design and its uses in creative collection development

- Recognize the importance of sampling ideas in the exploration and presentation of fashion

- Learn the steps involved in visualizing an original fashion collection

Design Processes

Translating a raw inspiration into a full range of fashion products is a challenging, rewarding, and exciting undertaking. The fashion industry thrives on imagination and innovation, and the primary role of a designer is centered on the ability to explore all possible creative avenues provided by a given inspirational starting point. While the important role played by original textiles has been discussed in Chapter 4, here we focus primarily on the steps taken to explore, visualize, and sample three-dimensional garments, as well as how these steps combine with textile options in the development of a fashion collection. The various tools and techniques discussed in this chapter provide a range of approaches for designers and **product developers** to implement in their design practice.

Designers and product developers, particularly those in training, should habitually document their creative exploration through the compilation of a design-development **process book** (sketchbook). The term "process book" will be preferentially used as part of this discussion, as thorough documentation of a collection-development process involves much more than sketches, and may include **collage**, images of original draping, detail sampling, photography, digital media, and much more.

Process books are valuable tools for showcasing a designer's creative abilities, and should always be considered as portfolio-worthy pieces. Design recruiters pay particular attention to process books because, while sketching technique and **construction** abilities are beneficial, creativity and experimentation are absolutely paramount for any role in design.

Opposite: Gestural sketching for silhouette and proportion exploration by Mengjie Di.

The three phases of design

Generally speaking, the development of creative ideas follows three phases: research investigation, design experimentation, and design refinement. Each one of these phases provides value and purpose to the final product, and should therefore be embraced.

1. Research investigation focuses on in-depth analysis of the research material. This phase does not yet involve visualizing garment shapes or details, but is instead directed toward extracting a broad palette of individual creative elements from the research, such as patterns, textures, lines, shapes, and colors. These individual items will then become the ingredients used in the next phase.

2. Design experimentation is the first venture into garment development. This phase makes use of the various individual research elements identified during the previous step, and explores a broad variety of possible applications and implementations. Various techniques are applied in this phase, such as collage, sketching, **digital draping**, and exploring volumes on the **form**. This is sometimes referred to as the "rough" design phase because the ideas being explored are not yet fully resolved.

3. Design refinement takes the best ideas developed during stage two and translates them into detailed visualizations. These will be used to edit the final collection and communicate with pattern-makers, cutters, sample sewers, and a variety of suppliers for the execution of garment prototypes.

While some designers may find it useful to pre-plan the process book, determining in advance what the focus of each section will be, others may find this approach overly restrictive. Documenting the three stages may work more effectively as an organic record of **ideation** and experimentation, as designers can develop ideas freely on loose paper, only compiling their work into a process book toward the end of the creative exploration.

Beyond the three phases of creative processing outlined above, designers must also ensure that they explore all of the various elements that will come together into final garments. These include the following:

— Silhouette/volume/shape
— Color
— Materials/fabrication
— Surface/pattern/texture
— Construction/details/finishings
— Styling/mood/creative context

Once again, these elements should not be approached in a segmented way, but should creatively feed off each other. For example, an idea pertaining to **fabrication** may inform an experimental concept for a closure, while the development of a piped material may guide the designer to investigate piped button loops as both a functional and esthetic detail. Similarly, an exploration of **pleating** may push you to reconsider how fabrics can give volume, which in turn may push you to redirect your approach to **silhouette**. Designers should allow these creative sparks to blossom.

Playful collage experiment by Ashley Whitaker, combining collected visuals, materials, and drawn elements.

Another important element to consider before launching into process-book development is that not all experimentation will produce a finished outcome. As a rule of thumb, only about 10 percent of initial ideas generated will translate into final looks. This means that when developing a capsule collection of, say, six looks, a designer should visualize between 60 and 100 possible outfits, each of which will likely be composed of multiple garments. With this in mind, all experimentation carried out should be recorded through the process book. The purpose of a process book is not only to present evidence of artistic talent, but also to showcase a designer's perseverance and commitment to exploring all relevant creative avenues.

Sketching, Collage, and Digital Media

Several tools can be used in the processes of research investigation, design experimentation, and design refinement. The most traditional approach employed by designers is fashion sketching, also commonly referred to as **croquis** sketching. While this style of sketching, used in visualizing design ideas on the human form, is an essential tool, it is not necessarily the best one to begin development. Designers jumping straight from raw research into croquis sketching tend to produce work that is overly limited by the physical shape of the body, interpreting the research in only the most obvious ways.

Two-dimensional approaches to process book experimentation should be diverse and playful so as to make the best use of the research gathered. They should include both manual and digital forms of observational analysis, image tracing, and collage, as well as croquis sketching.

Observational analysis and image tracing

To fully decode all usable elements gained from the raw research, designers carry out in-depth analysis of inspirational material through observational drawing and image tracing. By redrawing specific aspects of the research, they gain a deeper appreciation of their specific value and creative uses.

For example, if a designer is inspired by images of art deco architecture, the analysis of such material may involve isolating line patterns from the research, or identifying individual decorative elements from the collected imagery.

Two spreads from design process books by Fate Rising, blending drawing, collage, research imagery, and written notes.

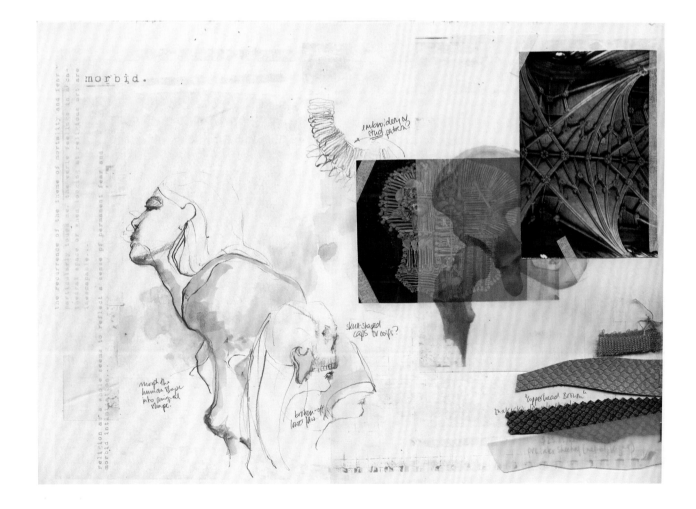

Top: Process-book pages by Fiorella Alvarado, combining research investigation and design experimentation, including textile play.

Above: Creative process by Jousianne Propp, exploring visual parallels between skeletal shapes and Gothic architecture.

Similarly, in a design project inspired by underwater sea creatures, the analytical investigation could take the form of close-up drawings or digital translations of particularly interesting shapes or surfaces.

Traditional approaches to drawing, including the use of graphite pencil, pens, markers, and wet media such as inks, watercolor, and gouache, can all provide valuable insights to the research. Each tool can reveal interesting and valuable aspects of the material at hand, so designers should explore diverse media and techniques as part of this process. At the same time, digital tools provided by graphic-design software, such as Adobe Photoshop or Illustrator, should not be overlooked, as they can open up interesting paths of exploration not normally fostered by traditional methods.

Collage

The technique of collage involves assembling various isolated pieces of visual research into a new creative arrangement. Collaging can be done by hand – by physically cutting up printed images or drawn elements from the research investigation – or digitally. The purpose of each combination of images is to provide one possible interpretation of how separate research components might interact together. Being able to record a wide array of collage experiments is essential, and one way to get multiple results from this technique if doing it by hand is to record each variation using a digital camera, rather than gluing the items down.

Exploring collage digitally has specific benefits not afforded by the traditional hand method. Digital tools allow the easy replication, scaling, and skewing of the individual elements being used in the collage process, which is very difficult to do without the use of computers, and can greatly improve the variety, complexity, and interest of the collage exploration. Collage can also be done using 3D objects, found items, fabric, ribbon, and yarn, and combining these with traditional and digital media. The possibilities are as diverse as the imagination of the collage artist.

Collaging is particularly helpful in two areas: exploring surface and experimenting with silhouette. Using collage as a tool for surface-pattern development can be done fairly freely. However, using it as a means for initial visualization of **apparel** or silhouette requires the inclusion

A collage experiment by Brooke Benson.

of elements that recall the human form. For this purpose, it is useful to supplement the visual research by collecting images of human body parts – arms and hands, legs and feet, and, most importantly, heads and necks. All of these will become reference points for understanding the collage experiment in relation to the standard human shape. When collating heads and faces to use in collage play, designers should be keenly critical of how makeup, hairstyle, and overall **styling** of these body elements may influence the result of the collage. Maintaining a certain level of neutrality in the styling can ensure the focus remains on the creative interest of the collage exploration, instead of being drawn to the face or shoes of the model.

Design experiments in collage by Amie Edwards.

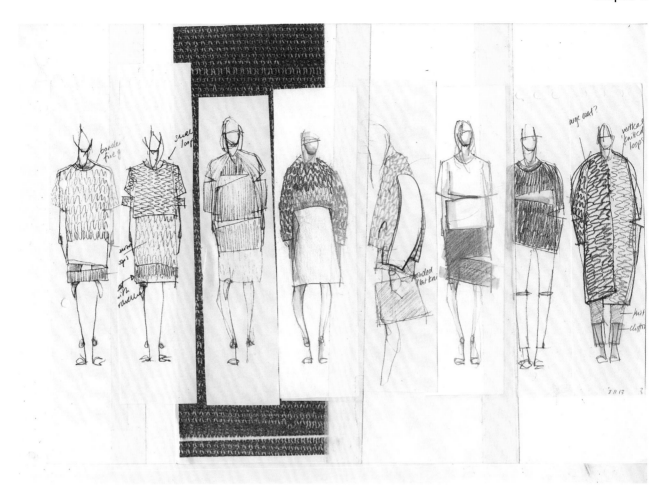

Design development through croquis sketching by Jousianne Propp.

Fashion sketching

Once research has been fully investigated and initial design experimentation has been undertaken, it may be time to visualize design possibilities on the human form. Traditionally done through fashion (or croquis) sketching, this approach provides a very effective way to communicate how an initial design might look when worn. To avoid confusion, it is essential to differentiate fashion sketching from **fashion illustration**. Illustrations are an important component of a final presentation for a fashion line, and therefore require quite a bit of care, attention, and time. Sketching, on the other hand, is intended as a quick visualization of creative possibilities. Most sketches take between two and five minutes to execute, for the simple reason that spending too long on them may turn out to be a waste of time if the ideas do not then become part of the final collection. Speed, in this case, can be a valuable friend, as it allows designers to envisage a vast number of possibilities and have a broad palette of design options at their disposal when it comes time to refine the collection. For the sake of consistency and readability, most croquis sketches are drawn in neutral standing or walking pose in order to communicate how the garment or outfit would appear in a runway presentation.

Croquis sketching also differs from fine-art sketching in not following realistic body proportions. Instead, it is based on an elongated, idealized human form. Taking the height of the skull as a basic unit, a normal human body tends to measure about seven to eight heads from the top of the cranium to the bottom of the feet. Fashion croquis, however, are lengthened (primarily by extending the limbs and neck) to measure at least nine heads.

The elongated croquis figure is intended to lend elegance and grace to the drawing. In croquis sketches of men, the lengthening is shared a little more evenly throughout the body than in women. Plus-size and youth croquis all follow slightly different proportional rules, but are still based on idealized forms. Some designers prefer sketching on highly stylized croquis figures, measuring 12–14 heads, which can provide a very extravagant feeling to the work produced, but tends also to affect the readability of the designs when moving to prototype development.

Of course, individual designers can choose to ignore the general rule of using a nine-head croquis. However,

This page: Gestural fashion croquis sketches by Mengjie Di.
Opposite: By playing with different media and proportions, fashion sketching can become quite experimental, as in these sketches by Elyse Blackshaw.

following the "standard rules" of fashion communication can have a positive impact on employability, as it will be more likely to meet the needs of fashion recruiters and established fashion companies.

While seasoned creatives are able to freehand their croquis sketches and achieve correct proportions each time, designers at the start of their training can use croquis templates to support the proportional consistency of their sketching. (A set of these for womenswear, menswear, plus-size, maternity wear, and children's wear is provided from page 200.) Tracing from a croquis template involves placing the chosen template under a plain sheet of paper, then drawing the garment or outfit over the croquis form. Tracing the croquis template itself should only be done on the parts of the body visible in the proposed outfit (hands, face, neck, and possibly lower leg). Every sketch, even a quick gestural croquis, should be given a sense of humanity. Hands, shoes, hair, and facial features make the sketches relatable as human beings, and help to envision the clothing design in a real consumer context.

E. Blackshaw

Exploring Silhouettes

Defining silhouette direction is of primary importance to any line, and should be tackled early on in the creative process. The silhouette is the overall shape and volume of the outfits making up the collection. While any collection will embrace a certain level of variety in the outfits included, the overarching approach to silhouette will present a sense of continuity for the sake of narrative consistency. Designers therefore define which silhouettes will be part of the collection and which will be excluded based on their inspiration, seasonal needs, market segment, and consumer type.

Unexpected silhouette play is a hallmark of the work of Comme des Garçons.

In experimenting with silhouette, designers should consider the creative potential of volume without being overly constrained by the physical shape of the human body, but being open to all relevant creative possibilities. This can be done through a multitude of methods, including collage, drawing, painting, and digital media. The task is to determine overall volume by focusing on how close or far from the body the garments might be. Using a croquis template as a starting point can be useful. However, because of the three-dimensional nature of silhouette, it can also be valuable to explore it from a variety of angles, or by using 3D-modeling software.

Common silhouettes seen in fashion:

— Square
— Trapeze
— A-line
— V-line or chemise
— Balloon or cocoon
— Column or sheath
— I-line or tubular
— Hourglass or bell
— Trumpet or mermaid
— Tunic

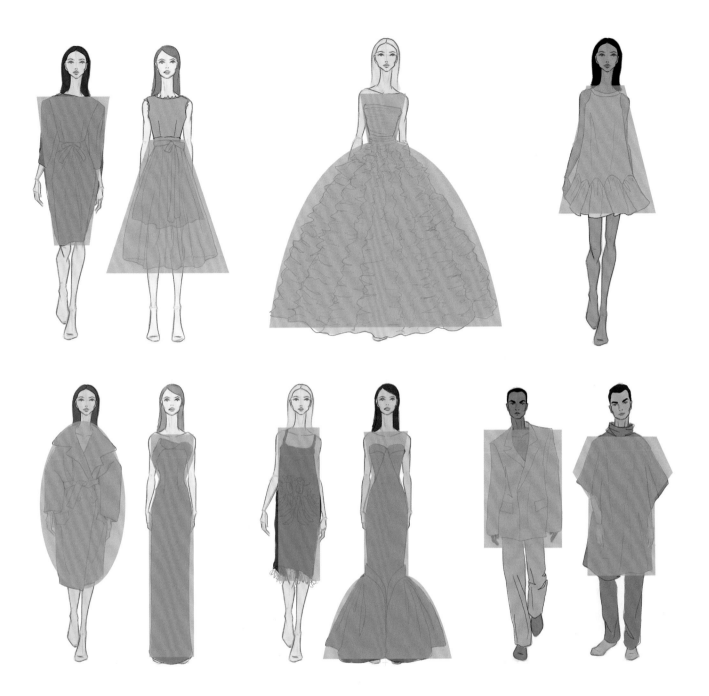

Key fashion silhouettes. From left to right: chemise, A-line, hourglass, trapeze, cocoon, column, I-line, trumpet, square, and tunic.

Certain markets and creative directions will lead naturally toward certain silhouettes: a mermaid silhouette is more likely to be seen in an eveningwear collection than a streetwear range. While seasonal and market expectations can inform a designer on which silhouettes are most likely to be appropriate for a certain collection, the creative decision rests ultimately in their hands.

While determining silhouette, designers should also be aware of a few common contextual implications. Certain shapes and volumes are seen as being heavily referential of specific historical time periods: short and tubular garments tend to recall the 1920s; long, hourglass shapes are reminiscent of the 1950s and the work of Dior; large, exaggerated shoulders bring the power dressing of the 1980s to mind. Using these visual connections intentionally can strengthen the **narrative theme** of a collection. On the other hand, a designer's lack of awareness of the way a certain silhouette is likely to be interpreted can lead to narrative dissonance and a final product that may end up confusing its intended audience.

Draping on the Form

Creative experimentation for fashion should be closely focused on the three-dimensional nature of apparel. Few ways of experimenting are better at addressing this than working directly on the dress form. Exploring garment possibilities by actively engaging with the human form can offer valuable and unexpected outcomes. Designers tackling experimentation on the form have a few different techniques available to them, including moulage, surface draping, garment fitting, **geometric pattern experimentation**, and **deconstruction**. Each of these approaches may be more or less relevant depending on the creative direction the collection is following. Additionally, designers can choose to work on the traditional full-scale dress form, or use half-scale forms, which, while retaining the required proportional accuracy, can be less cumbersome and require less fabric.

Moulage (from the French, meaning "molding") is the most traditional approach to draping on the form. This involves placing fabric on the **dress form** to produce the shape of a proposed garment. While moulage is normally done in cheap **muslin** (or calico), the draping quality of the material should reflect the behavioral properties of the intended final fabric. This means that moulage for a heavy overcoat, for example, will need to be done in a heavier muslin than that used for a light summer blouse. The purpose of moulage is to visualize a garment shape, refine its volume and silhouette, and explore the sculptural possibilities afforded by cloth. The results of moulage can be documented as part of a design process book, and can also be translated into working patterns for the development of garment prototypes.

Fashion moulage by Danilo Attardi.

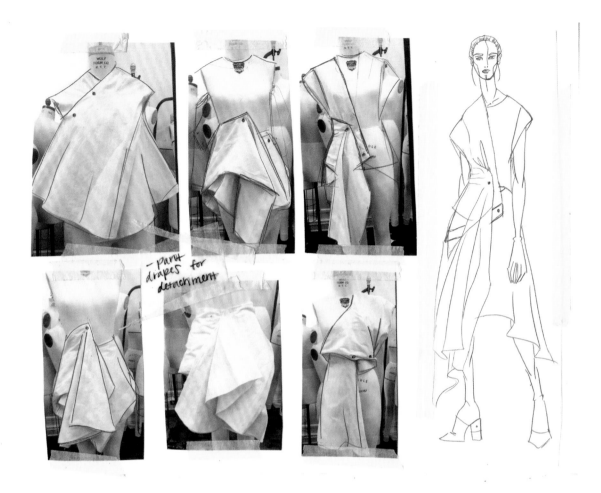

part drapes for detachment

Above: Draping on the form, recorded through photography first, traced over and then translated into a croquis sketch for enhanced readability. Process book page by Amanda Henman.

Right: Recording a draped experiment works best when combining photography, drawing, and notes, as in this example by Ariana Arwady.

Surface draping differs somewhat from moulage. While the latter focuses on visualizing the garment shape, surface draping is primarily concerned with the development of surface interest. This means that surface draping is usually a secondary process, after the shape of a basic supportive undergarment has been established. Surface draping is the technique employed to execute complex pleating, intricate smocking, or particularly elaborate ruching effects directly onto a garment in its three-dimensional form. Many designers, particularly those focused on eveningwear and *haute couture*, make extensive use of surface draping to add interest and craftsmanship to their work.

Garment fitting is the term used for reworking existing garments on a dress form, particularly by companies at the more commercial end of the marketplace, where design lines are unlikely to require highly experimental approaches to draping. Exploring collection ideas in this way can be quite effective, particularly for companies with a solid track

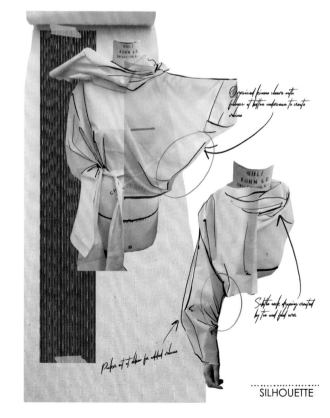

SILHOUETTE

Above: Deconstruction and reconstruction, a form of 3D collage, is used for this look by Erika Cavallini.

Left: Abstract shapes can transform into intriguing volumes and proportions, as in this geometric pattern experiment by Victoria Lyons.

record of sales in certain key styles and an established **brand identity**. This technique focuses on refining and tweaking the fit of garments from previous collections, or garments that may have been gathered from vintage stores, by carefully pinning seams and darts to achieve an improved outcome. The process of garment fitting is also extensively applied throughout the prototype-development stage, once the designs have been selected for production, in order to achieve the exact shape and fit intended.

Geometric pattern experimentation is a more experimental approach to draping on the form and is focused on pushing the creative boundaries of three-dimensional work. This approach requires the drafting of geometrically shaped patterns, such as complex polygons, spirals, and meanders, then cutting them out from paper or muslin. These pieces are then draped on the form to evaluate how the shapes can come together to form a garment. This type of method can generate highly imaginative results, which can be

virtually impossible to imagine through traditional croquis sketching. A similar approach is also employed in zero-waste garment designing, where the aim is to use 100 percent of the fabric length from which the garment is cut.

Deconstruction is another advanced experimental approach to draping on the form and is essentially a 3D version of collage. This technique requires taking apart existing garments from vintage shops or thrift stores, or perhaps unsold items from previous collections, and reassembling them on the form in new three-dimensional arrangements. This can be a very productive approach for designers interested in the environmental context of fashion garments, and wanting to develop new ways to upcycle apparel. On the other hand, deconstruction has been used extensively in the work of pioneering designers such as Martin Margiela, not as an environmental statement, but as a tool to question the conceptual boundaries of the fashion design process itself.

CAMERA PLACEMENT FOR EFFECTIVE
RECORDING OF DRAPED EXPERIMENTS

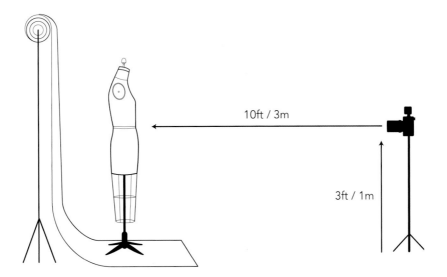

10ft / 3m

3ft / 1m

Documenting draped experiments

Regardless of the draping technique employed, the work produced will need to be properly documented and presented as part of the creative process book. Once again, breadth of exploration is important, and designers should push the range of their creative play, knowing that not all ideas explored on the form will result in final garments. When documenting work developed on the form, designers should ensure that the photographs taken are fully informative. Here are a few key pointers.

—   Photos should be taken against a plain background of a color contrasting with the fabric used for draping. If working in a light-colored fabric, the work should be photographed against a dark background and vice-versa. Setting up a backdrop specifically for this purpose in a corner of the studio can help a great deal.
—   Photography should take place in ample lighting so that all aspects of the work can be properly conveyed. Diffused natural light is best. Avoid spotlighting or "mood lighting," which can exaggerate shadows and make the imagery collected more difficult to understand.
—   Avoid perspective distortion. If taken from too close a distance, the resulting images can make parts of a garment look disproportionate and fail to convey the total appearance of the draped experiment. Take photos from at least 10 feet (3 meters) away, using the zoom function if necessary, and placing the camera about 3 feet (1 meter) above the floor (see above).

—   Given the three-dimensional nature of draped experiments, it is essential to photograph them from all angles. The dress form should be rotated and visually documentated every 45 degrees. This will give eight views for each experiment, which will be very useful should the look be chosen for further refinement toward a final garment selection.

In addition to photographic documentation, the process book will likely require drawings of the most effective draped experiments. These can start as traced line drawings from the photographic documentation, then be interpreted into a croquis format. Drawing can clarify certain design elements that might not be communicated as effectively through photography, and should be used to that effect.

While initial draping experimentation tends to focus mainly on creative exploration of design ideas, more refined drapes are often used toward the development of a set of working patterns. Accurate recording of such work is essential, as it will allow the original draped idea to proceed to the prototyping and production stages. Documenting an original drape for this purpose requires full photographic records, but also requires the designer to mark up the fabric while it is draped on the form. Once every **seam**, **dart**, gather, pleat, and fold has been marked, the item can be removed from the form and returned to a 2D format, which will then be transferred to pattern paper for future sampling and refinement.

Digital Draping

Many design approaches have blurred the boundaries of traditional sketching and process-book-based experimentation. Digital draping happens at the intersection of digital technology and three-dimensional design, when the capabilities afforded by computer software is effectively incorporated into 3D-design exploration.

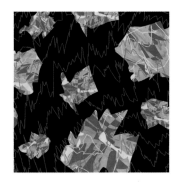

Above left: Original print design by Daniel Vedelago.
Above right: Digital draping variations by Denis Antoine.

The simpler forms of digital draping involve projecting imagery, photographs, or creative experiments directly onto the dress form or muslin garment. This can be used to explore the visual proportions of the looks under development and is essentially a life-size approach to collage. Each iteration can be photographed for future reference.

The Gerber technology suite offers a broad variety of tools specifically formulated toward the visualization of draped

shapes without ever needing to cut into fabric. The digital drape is structured over an avatar form customized to fit the measurements of the brand's customer, and can replicate the flow, movement, and sheen of virtually any fabric.

More advanced approaches to digital draping have been provided by technology such as Google's Tilt Brush, which enables designers to draw and paint digitally in a 3D virtual-reality environment.

Digital creation, making use of 3D-modeling software, by Hold.

Detail-focused Design

One of the key elements of effective design development is a focus on details. A vast number of successful garments and styles in the marketplace gain a superior reputation not because of the extravagance of their shape or the intricacy of their materials, but because of the value and refined execution of their construction details.

Some brands focus the majority of their design development on details, as this allows them to maintain a strong consistent brand identity while bringing slight innovation to each seasonal collection. These brands, including Tommy Hilfiger, Banana Republic, and Dockers, often adopt a creative methodology called **modular design**, in which the style is only altered, season after season, by choosing from a pre-established library of details, such as pockets, cuffs, collars, and **trims**.

Whether using details as part of a modular design approach, or incorporating strong details into an overall more experimental collection, designers must learn to visualize and communicate construction elements precisely and effectively. There are two main approaches to doing so: mock-ups and **technical drawing**.

Mock-ups, or sample prototypes, are a very effective means of exploring details as part of a design process. Mocking up pockets, closures, collars, and so on can provide a highly effective way of visualizing the specific technical variation, and evaluating if it will work within the collection or not. Mock-ups should be developed in stages, with the first throws being executed in mock-up muslin or another cheap fabric with similar properties to the intended final material. A final fabric mock-up should be executed only after the technical sample has been fully resolved in muslin, including very precise questions, such as the thread type to be used in topstitching, or the exact stitch length needed. While some mock-ups can be included directly in the process book, their physical size often requires them to be photographed, and the information gained from this process can be incorporated as one more component of the creative exploration. Original mock-ups can also be very useful for collage

Detail-focused look from Junya Watanabe Man, Spring 2018.

exploration on the dress form, experimenting with placement, scaling, and the overall density of detail use.

Technical drawings are an alternative to physically executing mock-ups of details under consideration. These can provide a useful visualization of details for both creative and qualitative evaluation. Technical drawings of construction details require in-depth analytical clarity and precision. They should be regarded as a means of communicating reality, so should offer fully resolved information about proportions, details, and functional elements. While initial sketches can be effectively worked out in pencil, the final technical drawing for communicating a garment detail tends to work best when cleaned up into a micron pen or Adobe Illustrator line drawing. This approach to technical drawing also forms the basis of design **flat drawing**, which will be discussed further in Chapter 6.

Technical drawing by Aitor Throup for C.P. Company, showcasing a variety of functional details.

Sampling Your Ideas

The fashion-design process is fundamentally a multisensory experience, as fashion products are, by their very nature, meant to connect to their consumers through various senses. Designers and product developers should therefore embrace this notion in their creative process, and go beyond croquis sketching. Any opportunity to bring ideas into physical samples throughout the creative process should be grasped. These will help a great deal in expressing the esthetic value of the exploration, and allow designers to make a better qualitative assessment of the ideas' viability for the finished line.

Alongside 2D research exploration, process books should include collage and sketching, actual samples of fabrics, surface experimentation, detail construction, and documentation of 3D experiments developed on the dress form. The combination of two-dimensional ideation and three-dimensional visualization will form the strongest basis for an effective, diverse, and multisensory creative process.

Including lots of physical samples in the process book can present certain challenges. For example, some samples may be too bulky or voluminous to display effectively in a **process book** format. In such cases, arranging these samples in a box can offer a suitable solution. However, it is important to include photographs of these sampled ideas in the process book so that the discoveries they present can be understood organically as they pertain to the rest of the ideation development. It can also be useful to label each sample, indicating which techniques were employed in its development, as well as providing a croquis sketch or design flat as a reminder of which potential design outcomes they may be connected to.

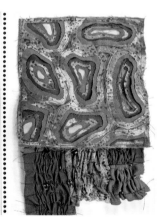

Process books by Caryn Lee.

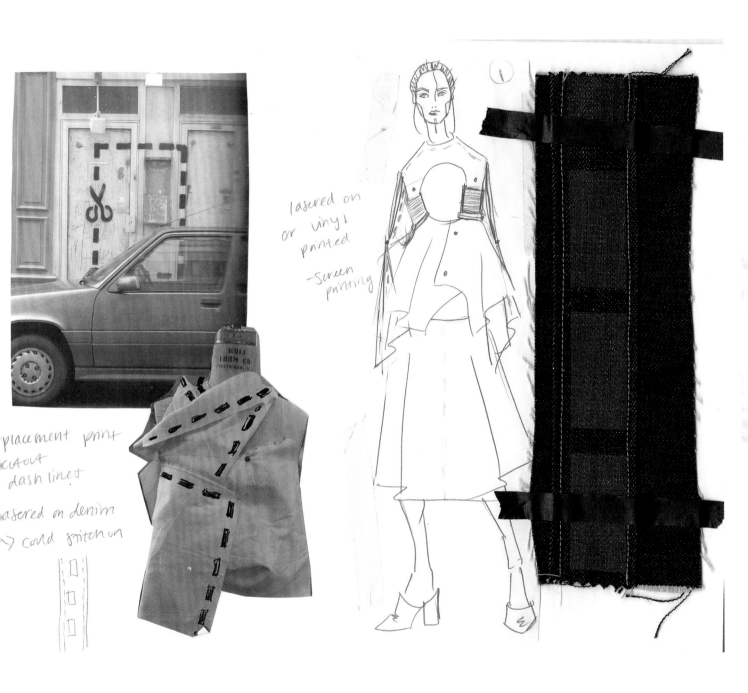

placement print
cut out
dash lines

lasered on denim
→ could stitch on

lasered on
or vinyl
printed

–screen
printing

Specific design details and finishes should always be sampled,
as in this example by Amanda Henman, for the most informed
and effective decision-making.

Visualizing Your Collection

Once all the possible creative ideas have been explored from the research, it is time to move into the design-refinement and collection-editing phase.

All the various design explorations coming from collage, draping, material exploration, and so on should be translated into fashion croquis format so they are visualized in a consistent manner. Individual creative experiments may lead to several iterations in croquis. For example, a certain surface manipulation may be placed in a multitude of different ways on a single garment, or may be implemented toward a variety of different silhouettes and garments. Each of these individual iterations should be rendered into a croquis format. In this step, designers should actively explore diverse garment options, as the variety of garment types generated at this stage will greatly help moving forward.

Styling

Once all your separate ideas have been rendered in croquis format, it will be much easier to style a collection. Styling in this case refers to the specific combination of items to form a variety of outfits, which will together read as a comprehensive and thought-out body of work. Many designers in industry develop garments individually, without committing them to predetermined outfits, which allows more creative play and inventive exploration through the process of styling. Subsequently, the editing of the collection is an exercise in selecting which of these garment combinations or outfits will generate the most valuable final outcome.

Below: Styling is all about combining individual garment ideas into complete outfits, and outfits into collections. This six-look capsule collection by Jousianne Propp carefully combines a variety of textiles, colors, textures, and garment types for an engaging outcome.

Opposite: Visualizing all possible outfit options for a collection. Artwork by Denis Antoine.

This page: A sharply edited capsule collection making strong use of volume and color, designed by Marina Meliksetova/Mélique Street.
Opposite: Croquis lineup by Eva Boryer.

The first step toward styling the collection requires the visualization of an ample variety of full outfits, bringing together all the separate design ideas developed through the design process. Careful attention to the needs of the intended consumer is paramount to the success of this task. Concerns such as the need for an outfit to provide insulation against the cold, or meet the basic requirements of functional wearability, will warrant more or less importance based on the specific consumer targeted. Going back to the **customer profile** established at the onset of the research and creative development can be of great benefit at this point.

When styling, designers should clearly define what purpose the outfits being developed will fulfill, whether these are intended to be directional showpieces or commercially substantiated looks. Indeed, designers who present themselves through their runway shows as experimental **design innovators** often develop separate lines of more commercially grounded product, commonly referred to as **diffusion lines**, for the sake of ensuring necessary cash flow for their business.

Editing

Once a wide array of complete outfits has been sketched into croquis, it is time to edit the collection. This is quite easily done by positioning sketched looks side by side to create a variety of proposed lineups. Here is where the advantage of digitizing sketches, or sketching croquis on loose pages, becomes evident. Having individual looks sketched separately allows the designer to move them around, and to remove or add looks as they see fit. This is also a point at which designers will be challenged to make tough decisions. Certain looks, which may be individually very exciting to the designer, may not work alongside the rest of the collection, and should therefore be eliminated. A designer may identify a problem in the collection, such as a need for more **separates**, or insufficient overall creative interest, which will require a return to the creative-exploration phase for further experimentation.

Another challenge involved in collection editing is to decide on color and materials. Although initial croquis sketches may be developed without color for the sake of focusing on the design shape and construction, the

process of editing requires the designer to identify how colors and materials will be employed throughout the collection. Redrawing individual outfit croquis in a variety of possible color combinations can be a great help in considering the multitude of options available.

Designers will usually visualize a variety of possible lineups, documenting each one in order to compare them side by side, and to best evaluate which of them ultimately presents the most effective creative solution. The final outcome of the collection-editing process is a color-rendered croquis **lineup** that includes all the necessary design information so that the work can effectively proceed to the design presentation and communication steps.

Designer Profile: Cucculelli Shaheen

Anthony Cucculelli and Anna Rose Shaheen are founders and co-creative directors of CUCCULELLI SHAHEEN.

Tell us about what made you want to be a designer.

Anna: I've been drawing since a young age, and my mother taught me how to sew. I would often buy vintage clothing and alter it.

Anthony: When I was in high school, I would alter my own clothing. I went to art school and then fashion school.

We felt there was a void in the marketplace for considered, thoughtfully made clothing that looked as beautiful in production as it did going down the runway. Even the luxury brands we were working for were always looking for ways to reduce costs and make more commercial product – which is not necessarily unimportant – but we were missing the romance and artistry of the process. By streamlining the production side, we are able to move quickly while keeping a very close eye on the workmanship, and we are also able to redesign the garments to match the client's proportions in the most complimentary way. Additionally, each fabric is dyed to dress order, so we do not sit on a lot of fabric inventory, as that is both wasteful and expensive.

Pattern-grading technology allows us to streamline our **supply chain**. Rather than doing multiple fittings, we're able to get an almost perfect pattern from the beginning. We adjust the pattern, then go straight to the final sample and do a fitting [of that] with the client – the way clothing used to be made before the mass-industrialization of the fashion industry. We also skip the in-between fitting processes by carefully grading and adjusting each client's patterns from the outset. We're taking what is normally a six- to nine-month process and delivering in four weeks.

How would you describe your brand?

We love the dichotomy of a very classical approach in the embroidery with the modern production process. We can design the embroidery to be most flattering for each client. Each collection is designed outside of the traditional fashion calendar and, once launched, remains open for customers and retailers to order from.

Why did you choose your specific niche? What opportunities has it provided you?

We love embroidery, detail, and pattern. By doing custom and made-to-order, we can incorporate all of these elements at a high level without compromising the workmanship. Part of our design process happens when we start to do the layouts on paper patterns – the artwork and colors often direct us to where the placements should go.

How do your chosen customer and market influence your design approach?

Many of our customers are brides, and are often outfitting for a week-long event – the rehearsal dinner, the wedding, something to dance in all night long! We also do a lot of red-carpet, gala, event dressing – women want to look beautiful and chic, but also fun and celebratory. We always keep in mind the end use when designing – can she move around, can she walk a red carpet and pose for photos and be comfortable in her skin? We strive for the client to wear the dress rather than the dress wearing the client.

A lot of our inspiration comes from travel, and we like to mix up our influences in each collection. Each dress has its own mini-mood board for layout and colors. At the same time, we are working on line drawings for the swatch pitches. We work a bit differently than ready-to-wear designers, as the swatch really directs what the dress shape will end up being.

We are constantly finessing our color and silhouette stories. We always have one or two last-minute launches that complete the story of the collection. As the collections

are small, we need to keep a balance of silhouettes as well, so we try not to repeat the shapes too much. The same goes for color, fabric, and motif movement.

What are the main challenges you have encountered while developing your business?

It was challenging at first to reach customers. Our dresses are expensive, and usually intended for a big event – customers want to feel confident that a beautiful garment will be delivered on time, and that they will look incredible, so can be reluctant to try a new brand. Now, approximately 30 percent of our clients are repeat customers.

How do you see the future of your segment of the industry?

We feel it is growing. As more luxury brands are trying to compete with the street-style brands, we are going in the opposite direction. With increased globalization, it's easier and easier for luxury customers to find what they are looking for. We are a New York-based brand, but our customers come from all over the world – we have a growing presence in the Middle East, Southeast Asia, Europe, and South America.

6. Presenting

a collection

Learning objectives

- Explore approaches to design presentation

- Understand the function and structure of a collection plan

- Identify the role played by fashion illustrations in the visual communication of a collection

- Evaluate the key technical considerations in developing strong illustrations

- Explore the technical approach to, and application of, flat and spec drawing in collection presentation

- Learn the practical steps necessary to compile range boards

- Gain familiarity with the function and structure of successful spec packs

Presenting Your Designs

For a collection to be successful, the work produced has to connect creatively with its intended audience. Designers must communicate their ideas in such a way as to appeal to design managers, buyers, and editors, who form the primary readership for new product lines. Effective design communication must showcase the collection's creative value, as well as convey all the necessary **construction** information needed to translate the **croquis lineup** into executed garments. This means designers are charged with the dual task of expressing their work both artistically and technically. Design presentation therefore needs to comprise elements that meet both of these requirements.

Prior to finalizing the line presentation, designers often employ a useful tool called the "collection plan." This organizes the entire collection into an easily manageable structure that can be used to direct all the subsequent steps of presentation and realization.

In order to present their work effectively, designers habitually make use of **fashion illustrations** and **technical drawings**, which will be the primary topics of this chapter. As a further step of design presentation, particularly when communicating with external pattern-makers and garment factories, designers also develop sets of production-focused information called **spec (tech) packs** (short for specification or technical packs).

Design presentation can make or break a collection, so is a critical step in the development of any designer's working practice.

Opposite: Abstracted watercolor illustration by Gabriel Villena.

Above: A design presentation board by Jousianne Propp, combining rendered croquis sketch, hand-drawn flats, and fabric swatches.

The Collection Plan

The creative process undertaken through the steps of design ideation and artistic experimentation discussed in previous chapters leads to a resolved lineup of color-indicated croquis sketches. This becomes the starting point for the development of a full collection plan.

All garments included in the lineup should be identified and grouped into categories. These include:

— Woven tops
— Woven bottoms
— Dresses
— Cut-and-sew knits
— Fashioned knits
— Tailoring
— Denim
— Leather
— Outerwear

The reason for separating a collection into these groups is that **manufacturers**, when producing the garments for **retail**, will most often contract a number of production factories, each specialized in a very narrow range of garment processes. Factories specialized in cut-and-sew knits, for example, are unlikely to also be expert tailors. Designers or manufacturing companies must therefore track each group of garments separately, based on the dedicated production steps required for those garments.

Another consideration to be aware of is that the success of any collection rests on whether buyers will, in fact, place an order from it. While showcasing the collection as full **styled** outfits helps convey the creative viewpoint of the designer, buyers are unlikely to purchase full outfits, and instead prefer evaluating the collection as individual pieces. Presenting the collection as a series of garments collated by **category** therefore makes it easier for buyers to order the pieces they feel best address their customers' needs.

The collection plan is established as a large chart listing each category and each garment within it, and gives each item a specific name or **style code** (see opposite). This code will then follow the garment through all stages of

prototyping, sales, and production. As part of the collection plan, garments are also visually communicated by using a **flat** or **spec drawing**, although the two terms have slightly different meanings. The term "flat" refers to a proportionally accurate line drawing of a garment, used in design meetings and collection planning, while the term "spec" refers to technical drawings used for communicating with production facilities in a spec pack. The technical requirements of these types of drawings are discussed later in this chapter (see page 153). The collection plan also often includes information pertaining to the size ranges being offered for each style, and the various materials in which they will be available.

For more commercially minded companies, establishing the collection plan can happen at the very outset of the creative process. In such cases, the collection plan forms a tool that designers use throughout the creative development so as not to waste effort or resources. This applies particularly to brands with a solid track record of sales in certain key categories. For example, The Row will consistently employ a collection-plan structure that includes many items of knitwear because this category is their best seller and it would therefore be counterproductive to change their product offering haphazardly from season to season.

While **design innovators** tend to focus their energy and creative efforts on the ideation of unique and exciting **apparel** items, they should also embrace the value of collection planning, as this can help them greatly in identifying areas of possible further expansion of the line for enhanced commercial success. This process is commonly referred to as **merchandising**. The role of the merchandiser is to assess lines in the context of their commercial viability, and to develop an assortment of products and retail strategies intended to improve the

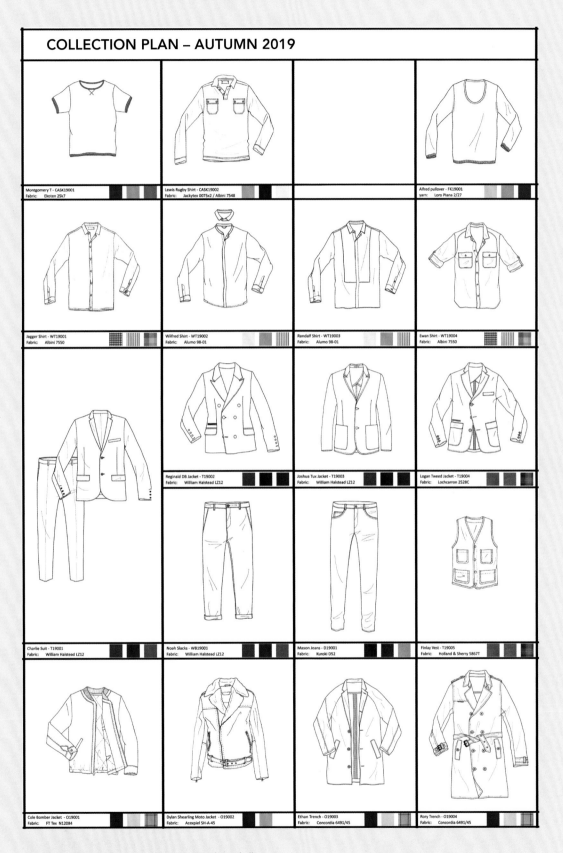

COLLECTION PLAN – AUTUMN 2019

Montgomery T - CASK19001
Fabric: Ekoten 25k7

Lewis Rugby Shirt - CASK19002
Fabric: Jackytex 0075x2 / Albini 7548

Alfred pullover - FK19001
yarn: Loro Piana 2/27

Jagger Shirt - WT19001
Fabric: Albini 7550

Wilfred Shirt - WT19002
Fabric: Alumo 98-01

Randalf Shirt - WT19003
Fabric: Alumo 98-01

Ewan Shirt - WT19004
Fabric: Albini 7550

Reginald DB Jacket - T19002
Fabric: William Halstead LZ12

Joshua Tux Jacket - T19003
Fabric: William Halstead LZ12

Logan Tweed Jacket - T19004
Fabric: Lochcarron 2528C

Charlie Suit - T19001
Fabric: William Halstead LZ12

Noah Slacks - WB19001
Fabric: William Halstead LZ12

Mason Jeans - D19001
Fabric: Kuroki D52

Finlay Vest - T19005
Fabric: Holland & Sherry 5867T

Cole Bomber Jacket - O19001
Fabric: FT Tex N12084

Dylan Shearling Moto Jacket - O19002
Fabric: Acexpiel SH-A-45

Ethan Trench - O19003
Fabric: Concordia 6491/45

Rory Trench - O19004
Fabric: Concordia 6491/45

A collection plan, showing each garment style and all
related fabric options.

Runway showpieces displayed at Viktor & Rolf Haute Couture shows
(right) inform the development of merchandised products **(left)**
carrying their label.

success of the brand. A directionally creative capsule
collection may therefore lead to the creation of further
items that are not always ideated directly within the design
team, but nonetheless convey the creative identity of the
brand to a wider audience.

An effective example of how this works can be seen in the
interrelationship between *haute couture* lines, designer
ready-to-wear (RTW) lines, and **diffusion lines**
(accessories, eyewear, cosmetics, and suchlike) within the
same brand. Creative direction is primarily established at
the higher end of the brand, through the work of the lead
design team for the *haute couture* and RTW shows, and is
later translated into broader arrays of commercially minded
products by the merchandising teams. This approach may
be applied within a single collection or across multiple

lines. In the first case, the creative vision for the collection
is established through **showpieces**, which are designed to
grab the attention of the press and the audience and tell
the story behind the collection. This vision then informs
merchandising teams in the development of the more
commercial products to be included in the collection, such
as knitwear or daywear pieces. In the case of design brands
offering multiple lines, the highest-priced line is usually
where the creative storytelling is at its most complex, and
that information is then used by merchandisers to develop
diffusion lines.

The collection plan, while primarily an internal tool for the
use of design, merchandising, and production teams, also
forms the basis for an essential collection presentation tool
called the **range board** (see page 158).

Illustrations

Presenting a collection of original designs requires the ability to communicate in creatively artistic and engaging ways. While designers in industry generally go straight from sketched lineup and collection plan to executing prototype garments, designers and students who develop custom apparel must usually present their idea to a client or review panel first in order to gain approval for the next phase of realization. Doing so can be challenging, and requires the careful and effective use of a series of techniques generally referred to as **fashion illustration**.

The term "fashion illustration" should not be confused with "sketching." The core difference between these two ways of visualizing fashion rests in their functional purpose. As discussed in Chapter 5, the intention of croquis sketching is to communicate design ideas in ways that, while somewhat proportionally enhanced, convey how the garments will look on the human body. Illustration goes further than that, in focusing more on creative storytelling and **editorial** narrative, and less on the specifics of what the clothing realistically looks like. This distinction can be difficult to grasp because many designers who work at the more commercial end of the marketplace commonly refer to a full body croquis sketch as an "illustration," and some illustrators talk of quick gestural illustrations as "sketches."

Lineups and design-presentation boards in a **portfolio** often make ample use of **rendered croquis** sketches, where more time and care has gone into color, shading, and texture than in standard croquis, which are sketched in just a few minutes. These rendered croquis convey the visual impact, fit, and materiality of the proposed garments and are therefore functionally equivalent to commercial fashion photography, as seen on most online retail platforms, which show the product in a neutral way for the sake of clarity.

A lineup of rendered croquis by Siting Liu.

Editorial fashion illustration by Gabriel Villena.

Editorial fashion illustration by Johnathan Hayden.

Illustrative format and composition

Choosing format and composition is essential in developing effective illustrations. Deciding whether a series of illustrations will be executed in portrait or landscape **page orientation** has a direct impact on their usability within a collection presentation or portfolio series. Also, choosing the overall size of the page to be used for these illustrations can impact subsequent media use. Working illustrations on a page that is too small will reduce the designer's ability to introduce detail, while a very large page format may be quite daunting and ill suited to media such as pen, marker, or pencil. In the process of presenting their work through illustrations, designers must consider format and composition in the same way as do painters, photographers, and other fine artists.

Determining the composition of illustrations before starting to draw is a very beneficial preparatory step. The composition of the work should be defined on the basis of how it will connect with and enhance the creative storytelling of the final illustrations, both individually and as a series (if multiple illustrations are being developed in one project). A useful way of doing this is to develop a thumbnail storyboard of all the illustrations being planned, visualized either side by side or in vertical alignment, depending on how the work will be ultimately displayed. In this way, composition elements can be carried through all the individual illustrations under development, strengthening them both individually and as a series. Composition types most commonly fall under two types: dynamic and geometrically formal. Each approach has potential benefits and disadvantages.

Dynamic compositions involve the use of irregularly placed elements, asymmetry, diagonal or curved lines, and the inclusion of items at multiple scales. This generates lively, playful works that are best for showcasing collections related to emotional stories and inspirations. Illustrations of collections originating from poetry, dance, or youth culture are likely to be well served by the use of dynamic compositions.

Editorial illustrations serve a very different purpose than rendered croquis. The focus of illustrations is generally driven by brand and collection narrative, so they tend to be used as replacements for editorial photoshoots by designers who are presenting a line but do not have actual prototype garments at hand. While showcasing product is still important, editorial communication, whether through illustration or photography, takes a more creative route, and in the process achieves an engagingly artistic outcome. Illustrating a collection requires awareness of both **brand identity** and the seasonal creative vision, and the implementation of media and artistic processes best suited to convey these. Illustrations are not restricted in format, composition, abstraction, or medium, and all these elements should therefore be carefully evaluated and implemented.

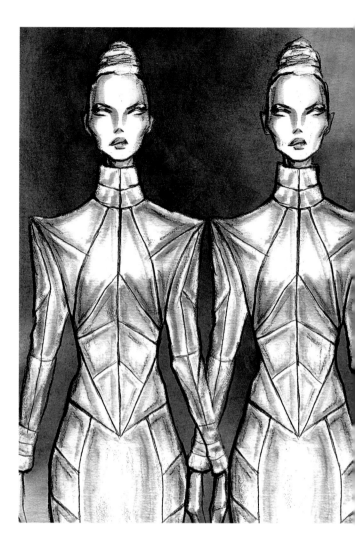

Above: This pen and marker illustration by Ashley Whitaker makes use of flowing lines and body positioning, to create a dynamic page composition.

Right: Lara Wolf employs sharp geometric formality in this composition, reinforcing the futuristic vibe of the garments.

Geometrically formal compositions, on the other hand, rely on structure, organization, symmetry, and regularity. The very nature of these compositions generally communicates a sense of control and absence of sentiment. Collections inspired by minimalism, architecture, or emotional distance can benefit from illustrations structured around geometrically formal compositions.

Illustrative media and abstraction

Just like fine artists, fashion illustrators should not be limited by specific media choices. Designers and illustrators should select media based on two primary considerations: whether the medium is able to articulate the subject matter effectively, and whether the media used communicate the mood of the collection. In many ways this can be a challenging choice to navigate, as a particular

medium may be great for visually communicating a certain material, but detract from the expressiveness of the work in its totality. Illustrators should allow for sampling of techniques in order to make the best-informed choices in terms of media use.

The textural qualities of the collection being illustrated can provide an effective guide as to which media are useful to explore. For example, denim traditionally requires a medium with a grainy texture, such as color pencil or crayon. On the other hand, satins and other glossy materials are most commonly rendered by using wet media, such as watercolor, gouache, or marker. Experimenting with media combinations, mark-making, and digital play are highly beneficial in the process of selecting effective tools and methods.

Unlike rendered croquis, which tend to follow a much more structured set of rules, illustration allows designers to play

Media play and abstraction can lead to intriguing and artistic results, as in this illustration by Nataša Kekanović.

Above: Illustration by Gabriel Villena, combining realistic and abstracted elements through the choice of media.
Right: Alina Grinpauka blends realistic line details in facial features and garment elements, with broadly abstracted use of color.

much more freely with format, composition, media, and abstraction. Abstraction in this case refers to how far the images may veer away from realism for the sake of expressiveness. Full realistic execution may not always be the most suitable approach, as it is often very time-consuming and can detract from the emotional communication of the work. This can frequently be seen in the way fashion illustrators approach the human face. While employing a fully realistic illustrative technique communicates what the person looks like, it can sometimes feel overly precise or formal. A simpler approach, in which faces are distorted, stylized, or merely suggested by a few lines, can be better at communicating the humanity and emotions of the subject. Yet again, sampling multiple approaches, from the most realistic to the most abstracted, allows an illustrator to make the best choices for communicating seasonal inspiration, mood, and brand identity.

Drawing Flats and Specs

While some designers develop collections by visualizing garments and outfits as croquis sketches, many design teams prefer to communicate using flats or specs. The difference between a flat drawing and a spec drawing rests in the purpose of each approach. Flats are proportionally accurate line drawings of garments that are used in design meetings and collection planning so that the exact appearance of each garment can be fully understood by everyone present. Specs, while based on a very similar line drawing, tend to focus in greater depth on what factories need to know for production purposes, and can therefore involve more technical elements, multiple views, detail close-ups, internal structure, and so forth.

Both flats and specs are grounded in proportionally accurate line drawings. This means that if all the garment prototypes for a collection will be developed in a US size 6, the flat template should reflect the exact proportional qualities of a standard size 6 **dress form** or fit model. Designers can easily develop their own flat templates. One way of doing this is to select the standard sample size for the line, and then photograph the dress form (ideally with legs and arms) of the chosen size. The photograph should be taken from a minimum distance of 12 feet (4 meters), with the camera place approximately 3 feet (1 meter) from the ground, to avoid possible proportional distortion. This photograph can then easily be traced, indicating the body outline and the main reference lines, including chest, waist and hip, center-front and center-back lines. For ease of reference, flat templates based on a standard US women's size 6 (UK 8, European 36) and a standard US/UK men's size 38 (European 48) are included at the end of this book (see page 200).

Flats can be drawn by hand with a mechanical pencil and micron pens, or by computer, using vector-based graphic software such as Adobe Illustrator. Each approach has potential benefits and pitfalls. Drawing flats by hand tends to be quick, but rendering proportions and fit accurately does require practice. Digital flats, commonly employed in mass-market and mid-level brands, are executed on a computer screen, which allows easier editing, refining, and tweaking by multiple team members, and across multiple seasons in the case of carryover garments. However, they can lack softness and appear overly stiff.

The basic rules of proportional accuracy, line quality, and detail are the same for all flats. The thickness and type of line used communicates the garment details. Commonly, the outline of flats is drawn with the thickest line, medium-thickness lines are used to indicate folds, vents, or drapes, and thinner solid lines are employed for seams. Topstitching is drawn as a dashed line.

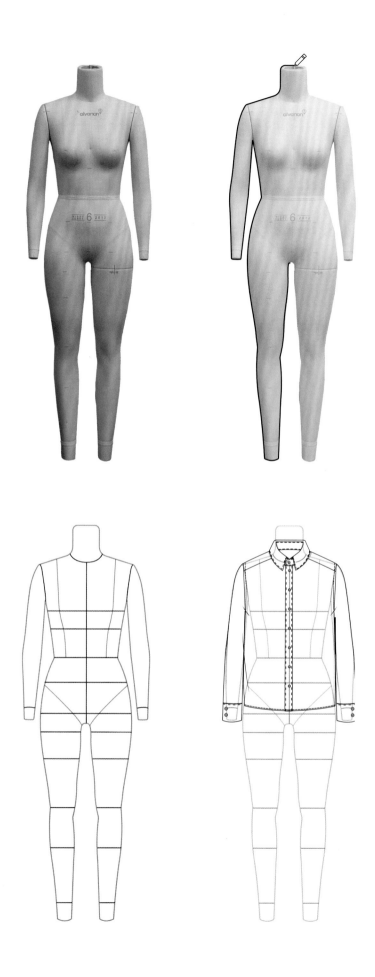

Developing a flat template from a photograph of a dress form, and using it for flat drawing.

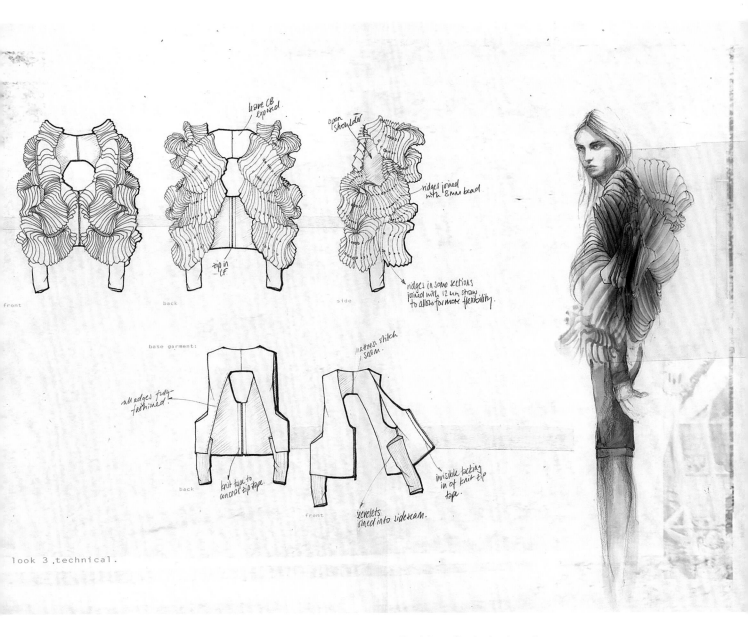

Hand-drawn flats by Jousianne Propp.

Drawing flats by hand

1. Trace in pencil

Select and magnify the correct flat template, then draw the garment in pencil on a sheet of layout paper placed on top of the template. Take care to establish the overall shape, main seam lines, drape, and closures. Flats drawn too small run the risk of lacking detail, so a rule of thumb is to opt for a minimum size of 5 x 5 inches (13 x 13 cm), as flats can always be digitized and scaled down later as needed. Make careful considerations of fit, volume, and ease, as very few garments sit directly on the skin of the wearer.

2. Trace using pen

Once the pencil drawing is completed, place another sheet of layout paper on top of it, or use regular drawing paper on a light box, and trace the drawing cleanly, using pens.

3. Add shade

Shading is not always required, but can be added using light-gray marker to indicate either some sense of volume, or the inside of the garment (for example the back neck area when looking at a shirt from the front, or the back hem area of a high–low skirt).

155

Drawing flats digitally

1. Import a template
Digitize and import the flat template into the software platform being used.

2. Add lines
Use line tools to visualize the look. Take care to use line qualities that will maintain a sense of materiality and flow.

3. Add stitching and details
Software such as Adobe Illustrator makes it easy to set up a regular dashed line that renders visible stitching much more cleanly than by hand. One major advantage of working digitally is that you can develop "brushes," or automated swatches, for things such as zippers, closures, and **trims**. In the long run, this makes the digital approach much faster than hand-drawing.

Ultimately, all flats should be truly elegant line drawings, avoiding unnecessary stiffness, to reflect the flow, fit, and appeal of the garments being communicated. They should also include all the construction details of a garment, such as seams, visible stitching, gathers, pleats, buttons, zippers, ruffles, and so on. Essentially, it is important to show anything that is sewn or has a clear three-dimensional quality – for example, the texture of fur or cable knitwear. For ease of reference, examples of flats are included at the end of this book (see pages 206–13).

One thing that does not generally appear in flats is color. This is because the same flat will be used to develop a **production run** of the item, which may include multiple color options involving both solid colors and printed materials. The flats should therefore be kept as clean line drawings until the final range offering is established.

A good flat will often become the starting point for the development of spec drawings, which will add to the information contained in the flat by providing extra detail, close-up views, internal views, and anything else the factory would need for the purposes of production.

Digital flats by Johnathan Hayden.

Compiling the Range Board

The range board is a very useful tool that enables buyers to see all the garments being offered in all available material options. This is commonly included in a design presentation in order to reinforce the designer's responsiveness to the needs of buyers, and also to provide a better sense of how the capsule collection showcased in a lineup may expand into a broader range of interesting options.

Preparing an effective range board requires two key elements: a full set of flats for all garments in the collection, and a full assortment of fabrics, grouped by apparel category (shirtings, suitings, coatings, **bottom-weight fabrics**, and so on).

The next step is to create copies of each garment flat in each of the colorways that will be offered. For example, if a jacket will be available in four different materials or colors, four copies of the same flat will be needed.

Each copy should then be filled in with the color and/or texture of the material it will be made in. For solid colors, using the "color fill" or "paint bucket" tools on Adobe Photoshop or other design software is a quick solution. For patterned or textured materials, it is best to digitize the fabric and place it in the flat digitally. Of course, within any given garment category, fabrics will repeat across items. For instance, different styles of shirts are all likely to be made available in the various shirting fabrics selected for the line.

When developing the range options, designers should try to keep a balance between solid and patterned fabrics, and between staple colors (neutrals, grays, black, white, and navy) versus directional **seasonal colors**. This consideration should apply within each apparel category, as well as across the entire line. Appealing to buyers is best done by providing a variety of options demonstrating awareness of consumers' needs.

The visual presentation of the range board is commonly done by placing all the garments in category groupings, and showing every fabric variation for each style by laying out all the respective filled flats together, slightly overlapping, and aligned diagonally. This layout is commonly referred to by design teams as a "waterfall."

The various filled flats developed for the range board are also frequently used by the brand's marketing and sales teams to develop the line catalog, an important document used during trade-show presentations to buyers.

CARGO/FIELD JACKET
WITH PATCH POCKETS
AND WAIST BELT

ROUNDNECK TEE
SHORT SLEEVES
100% COTTON

SAFARI SHIRT/BUSH SHIRT WITH
EPAULET ON SHOULDERS
AND SLEEVES

HUNTING VEST
WITH PATCH POCKETS
THICK RIB ON ARMHOLE
AND BOTTOM HEM

HENLEY NECK
SHORT SLEEVES

POLO SHIRT
SHORT SLEEVES
YARN-DYED

A range board for a men's sporting collection, showing each
style in every fabric option available.

Spec Packs

In the fashion industry, the production of garments is most often contracted to factories rather than being executed within design studios. While showpieces, which are intended to display the creative capacity of the designer and the inspiration behind the collection, are often realized under close control of the design team, the vast majority of items within the line are sampled by contractors, who will later oversee the ultimate production run if the style is selected by buyers. Working with external production facilities requires precise communication tools called spec or tech packs. The information these contain is put together in a way intended to reduce misunderstanding, and must include every possible detail needed by a production team (often located many thousands of miles away) to fully understand all aspects of the design.

The spec pack commonly includes various sections, each of which focuses on a slightly different element of production-relevant information.

General style information: This is usually presented as a cover page to the spec pack, and includes front and back flats, **style code** or tracking code, and available sizes and colorways. The basic style information will also be included in a header running on all subsequent pages in the spec pack.

Chart of materials, trims, and findings: This chart lists every material to be used in the construction of the apparel item, from outer fabric to lining, interfacing, shoulder pads, thread, buttons, zippers, and any decorative trims. Each material, trim, and **finding** must be listed with specific information about the supplier, the product-reference code needed to source it, and an indication of the required quantity and associated price. Keep in mind that the material style may be available in a variety of colors, so precise information is paramount.

Specification drawings: This section of the pack presents all the necessary visual information needed to fully understand the style. For simple garments, one page may be sufficient, but intricately detailed items may require multiple pages. As mentioned on page 153, specs include, whenever necessary, detail views, internal construction views, close-ups, and any other visual information required for full documentation of the item. These are generally presented with all associated measurements, such as pocket width, collar depth, and label placement.

Key control measurements: One page of the spec pack is usually dedicated to listing key garment measurements. For pants, for example, these would include the length of the inside leg seam, plus the seat and waist circumference, while jackets and shirts would specify the chest and waist measurement, and the length of the center-back seam, shoulder seam, and sleeves. The more specific the measurements, the better. They will ensure that the garments sewn by the production team meet the specific expectations of the design team. Since garment

Spec pack pages by Nikki Kaia Lee.

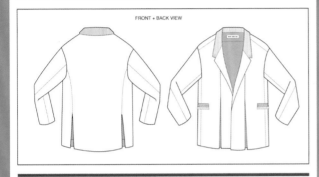

STYLE # TE2017	SIZE RANGE: WOMEN'S 0-10
STYLE NAME: DROPPED COLLAR JACKET	FABRICATION: 100% WOOL SUITING / 100% NYLON TULLE
SEASON: SS//2018	SAMPLE SIZE: SIZE 6

FRONT + BACK VIEW

SPEC MEASUREMENTS

A.	BODY LENGTH	30"
B.	CHEST (1" BELOW ARMHOLE) CIRCUMFERENCE	56"
C.	WAIST	54"
D.	BOTTOM SWEEP	59"
E.	SLEEVE LENGTH	25.5"
	BICEP	18.5"
	ARMHOLE (CURVED)	25"
	SHOULDER DROP	2"
I.	NECK OPENING	15"
	COLLAR HEIGHT AT CENTER BACK	2.75"
K.	POCKET WIDTH	5"
L.	WELT POCKET LIP HEIGHT	.75"
M.	PLEAT LENGTH	12"

FABRICS
100% NYLON TULLE / 100% SCREENPRINTED WOOL SUITING

FRONT VIEW

SPEC MEASUREMENTS

	BODY LENGTH	30"
	CHEST (1" BELOW ARMHOLE) CIRCUMFERENCE	56"
	WAIST	54"
	BOTTOM SWEEP	59"
	SLEEVE LENGTH	25.5"
F.	BICEP	18.5"
G.	ARMHOLE (CURVED)	25"
H.	SHOULDER DROP	2"
	NECK OPENING	15"
J.	COLLAR HEIGHT AT CENTER BACK	2.75"
	POCKET WIDTH	5"
	WELT POCKET LIP HEIGHT	.75"
	PLEAT LENGTH	12"

BACK VIEW

GARMENT DETAILS
"EMBROIDERED" COLLAR

NIKKI KAIA LEE

TOP COLLAR IS OVERLAID WITH A LAYER OF TULLE, AND BETWEEN THE LAYERS PLACE THE FOLLOWING:
-9 LARGE SILVER SEQUINS
-7 SMALL SILVER SEQUINS
-27 SEED BEADS
-15 BUGLE BEADS

BEADS WILL SHIFT IN BETWEEN THE LAYERS: DO NOT PHYSICALLY SEW THEM IN

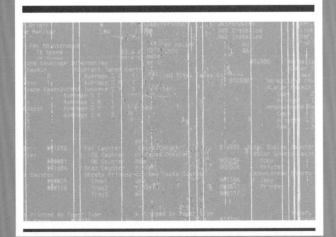

COLOR WAY OPTIONS

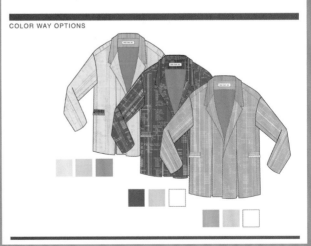

Presenting a collection

The Christopher Raeburn sample room, where design ideas become prototypes. Designers must communicate effectively with sample-makers and production facilities to avoid costly mistakes.

construction is performed by human beings and is therefore prone to slight variation, all measurements should be listed with an indication of the allowable **tolerance** – the acceptable measurement discrepancy between the sample garment and the items generated in the production run. A measurement listed as 32in Tol. ±¼ indicates that the ideal dimension is exactly 32 inches, but garments measuring anywhere between 31¾ and 32¼ inches will be accepted by the **manufacturer**.

The chart of control measurements is often expanded to reflect how each of these measurements and tolerances will change for each size the garment will be produced in. This is sometimes referred to as a "sizing chart."

Construction operations: For maximum clarity, the spec pack can include a full step-by-step listing of construction operations to guide the production team. Each sewing step is listed in the exact order required. Each seam, trim, and closure process is briefly described, along with a diagram of how the fabric layers are to be assembled. The information also indicates the type of machine, thread, and stitch length needed for each step.

Material information: Garments requiring specific printing, manipulation, or **embellishment** processes can be described in full technical detail in a dedicated section of the spec pack. Other useful elements of this information include sample photographs, technical drawings, listing of process steps, and exact Pantone color references.

Costing: Spec packs can include an initial breakdown of cost. The costing is calculated for each individual garment within the production run, so while some costs, such as materials and trims, will be directly informed by the style itself, others, such as the cost of shipping, pattern development, and grading, are one-off fees that are divided by the number of garments in the run.

Costing should include a breakdown of:

— Material costs, based on the specific amount of fabric, trims, and findings required.
— Pre-production costs, including patterning, grading, marking, and cutting.
— Production costs, listing the exact fee charged by the **contractor** for assembling each garment.
— Other costs, such as **packaging**, shipping, and import tariffs.

Estimating production costs

All of the bulleted items above add up to the cost of production, which is usually about half of the **wholesale** *price, itself likely to be doubled by stores to arrive at the final retail price. Thus, a garment that cost $15 to manufacture will usually have a wholesale price of $30, and retail around $60.*

Accuracy in initial costing can be especially important to some labels at the lower and middle segments of the marketplace. These companies often use initial costings to decide whether a style will be produced, as items that do not fit within the standard pricing range of these brands will usually be removed from the line.

A note on realization

In-depth knowledge of garment construction is essential for designers, as it informs their creative choices, from concept to spec pack. Indeed, students of fashion often spend vast amounts of time realizing their designs as **muslins** *(or toiles) and final prototypes. However, it is important to be aware that most of the construction work in the fashion industry is not done directly by designers. That said, designers must demonstrate complete comprehension of construction, as they are ultimately responsible for supervising, guiding, and finally approving the work of sample-makers, pattern-cutters, and production specialists.*

7. Portfolios and résumés

Learning objectives

- Consider the presentation of a portfolio of creative work

- Create a brand vision and communicate it to an audience

- Understand the audiences with whom young designers need to communicate

- Evaluate effective layouts used in the visual presentation of portfolio work

- Consider digital portfolio-presentation platforms, and the opportunities they provide

- Identify the key components of successful résumés

- Develop interview skills needed to present design work successfully

Portfolio Presentation

This chapter focuses on the steps involved in bringing creative design work to an industry-ready presentation. Young designers entering the fashion industry do so by developing a **portfolio** of work intended to showcase their creative and technical skills. The portfolio is a packaged, edited collection of projects that can take the form of a physical book or a digital presentation. Young designers should start building a portfolio from the outset, recording their design projects in a consistent and intentional way, with a particular focus on the audience they wish to connect with, namely fashion recruiters.

The creation of an effective portfolio requires a certain level of pre-planning, both in the presentation of each individual project to be included, and in the overall packaging of the entire body of work. Designers should always start by determining a brand vision for themselves, as this will pervade each and every project undertaken, and should speak clearly throughout the portfolio. Once this has been established, communicating the brand vision will involve making certain key decisions about tools of visual communication, such as **logo**, use of color, graphic-design elements, and overall layout choice, all of which will be discussed in this chapter.

Industry preparedness involves far more than being a talented designer. All aspects of presentation work hand in hand, and a strong candidate for employment must therefore demonstrate professional communication abilities in their **résumé** and job interview.

Right: Portfolio presentations at ITS (International Talent Support) 2018, a leading international fashion talent competition.
Opposite: Portfolio book by Aitor Throup.

Creating a Brand Vision

The best tool for developing a purposefully focused portfolio of work is a clear brand vision. While brand direction in relation to marketplace positioning for a new line is addressed in Chapter 2 (see pages 33–35), here the focus is on personal branding, as required for effective and consistent communication.

Early on in their professional training, young designers should determine which professional role, market segment, or key garment categories of interest they wish to pursue. It is perfectly normal to struggle with identifying a personal niche. The simplest way to get a sense of what you want is to ask yourself, "What makes me happy?"

Once a designer finds the specific type of work that gives them deep personal satisfaction, be it pattern cutting for the **better** or **moderate** market, textile development for designer runway, or couture tailoring design, all the other considerations of personal branding will follow naturally.

The next step in developing a personal brand vision is to draw up a list of core-value terms relating to the personal **niche**. A young professional focused on pattern cutting for **high street** brands might embrace terms such as "approachable," "technical," and "modern," while another focused on couture-level design might select words such as "artistic," "extravagant," or "luxurious." These core-value terms can then be formulated into a simple sentence that will become somewhat of a personal mantra for the design professional, and form the foundation of all visual communication and portfolio presentation. For example, "My work offers artistic visions of fashion, bringing luxury materials and surrealistic creative processes together." The personal brand-vision statement is also likely to guide the individual's approach to the design process and collection development itself across all projects undertaken.

Logos, packaging, color, and graphic design are all used as part of portfolio presentation to communicate the personal brand vision, and should clearly strengthen the individual's creative direction in the eyes of the portfolio's audience.

Developing a logo

The logo is the first graphic representation of your personal brand. Logos play an important role in our industry because all forms of commercial branding center on the brand logo. For instance, the orb has become synonymous with the work of Vivienne Westwood, and the YSL logo is intrinsically tied into the Yves Saint Laurent brand in all its embodiments. Developing a strong logo for a new creative voice in our industry can be both valuable and challenging.

A strong logo should effectively communicate the brand values or brand vision without any need for explanation. While many logos focus on the designer's name, some communicate in non-verbal ways. For example, the famous Nike "Swoosh" logo clearly speaks to the brand's focus on motion, speed, and positivity. Even brands focused on verbal communication make intentional use of **typography** to communicate the brand's values. With its clean sans-serif font, the logo of TopShop communicates approachability and modernity, while the logo for Alexander McQueen extols the brand's luxury and historicism by making use of a more complex serif typeface. Determining the look of a logo for a personal brand should therefore start with clarity of vision and values, and the logo design should be assessed on the basis of how effectively it communicates your chosen message.

Key factors in effective logo design include:

Simplicity of images or typography: A good logo should be usable on everything from labels to business cards and storefront signage. The variety of formats the logo will need to be applied to makes it particularly difficult to include very intricately detailed imagery or typography.

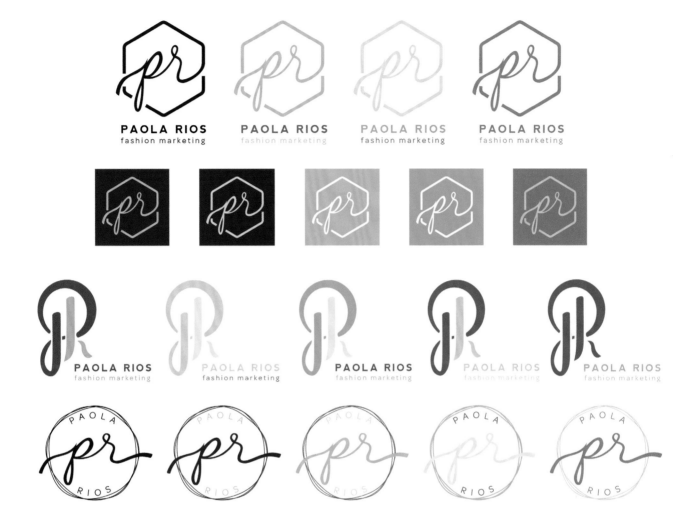

Logo-design development by Paola Riós.

Readability: The purpose of the logo is to be understood instantly by its viewer. It is therefore important to avoid designs that use graphic-design elements or abstraction in ways that hinder the clarity of the content and message.

Appropriate use of color: Color plays a pivotal role in communicating brand values. Some brands benefit from a playful esthetic, while others are best embodied in a minimal, black-and-white design. For example, hot pink is perfectly well suited to Betsey Johnson or Accessorize, but would be entirely off-key for a brand such as Dior. Another consideration is that most logos in the fashion industry are designed so that they can be easily woven into garment labels. Inevitably, this limits the number of colors that can be used simultaneously while maintaining reasonable cost-effectiveness.

Successful brand messaging: The core challenge of any logo design is how it will convey the brand. Poor logo design can convey values that differ from those central to the brand itself, or – even worse – fail to convey any meaningful message at all. If a designer wants to present their work as luxurious, but their logo primarily communicates a sense of homespun handicraft, their brand message is seriously undermined.

All of the challenges and common pitfalls listed above can be easily navigated by seeking out opinions during the logo-development process. Gathering feedback from as many people as possible is very worthwile, and using social-media platforms to do so can be particularly valuable. Take note that collating and acting on feedback is an integral part of any design work.

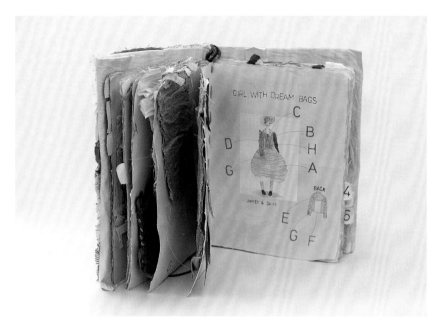

Left: Craft bookbinding techniques and tactile materials combine effectively in this experiential portfolio booklet by Momoko Hashigami.

Opposite above: All elements of branding should work together across media and formats, such as in this press pack and portfolio book for Azede Jean-Pierre.

Opposite below: A series of portfolio pages by Kevin Warwick, showcasing all aspects of design ideation, inspiration, development, and collection details.

Packaging

Packaging is as important as logo design in communicating brand values, both in the context of commercial brand and personal creative identity. The parallel with **retail** in this case is clear, and young designers should remain aware that recruiters, buyers, and any other professionals they interact with are used to perceiving brands through packaging on a daily basis.

Material and color choices are, of course, central to effective packaging. While a sharp, clear acrylic box may be brand-relevant for some, a hand-bound, embossed leather folder may be more suitable for others.

Packaging approaches to portfolio presentation tend to fall into two general categories, books and boxes.

A bound format tends to be easier for the audience to navigate, but it can be limiting when presenting to a large group. It is important to choose a binding that allows the designer to add or remove pages for greater relevance to a specific audience. For this reason, many portfolios use books with screwpost binding.

The advantage of presenting a portfolio as a box of separate pages or boards is that it can be shared and looked at by multiple viewers simultaneously. However, this very flexibility can make it trickier for the presenter to control the order in which the work is viewed. Box presentations tend to be more conducive to showcasing large textile swatches, voluminous samples, or 3D mock-ups.

Some designers may choose to combine both formats, presenting their main design work as a book, and adding samples and mock-ups in a secondary box.

Commercially available portfolios come in a variety of materials, including bamboo, acrylic, aluminum, leather, and cork. Most of these can be easily customized through engraving or laser-cutting to showcase the designer's logo or some other engaging visual material.

Rather than buying portfolio books or boxes, some designers choose to explore bookbinding processes and to produce unique, hand-crafted presentations. Once again, the choice should be made on the basis of its relevance to personal brand values.

It is important to be aware of the sheer quantity of portfolios a recruiter will see over the course of any given day. It is therefore vital to catch their attention with a unique and personal presentation. Strong packaging should engage the intended audience even before they see the actual design work, making them feel the brand message and impressing them with the care and attention placed in the work. Packaging choices should inform all brand communications, from portfolios to **lookbooks**, and from résumés to greeting cards. Consistency is key to effectiveness.

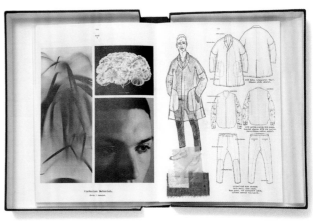

Understanding Your Audience

A standard presentation of a single design project as part of a portfolio format usually includes the following elements.

Cover page: This sets the stage. It is best not to date a collection, but instead just give it a title. This will make the work relevant for a longer time.

Inspiration/concept board: A visual summary of gathered visual inspiration.

Mood board: A presentation of the emotional direction of the collection developed.

Customer profile: A clear lifestyle-focused visualization of the ultimate consumer intended for the line.

Colors: These should be presented as a **color palette** or **color bar** with specific Pantone referencing. It does not have to be a separate page, but can be introduced as a section of a previous board.

Process: A visual summary of the creative process undertaken in the development of the collection. This can be done by digitizing some of the stronger **process book** pages, or by creating a **process collage**.

Materials: Physical swatches of original and source materials, as relevant.

Lineup of rendered croquis: Often showcased across a full spread of the portfolio, the lineup presents the collection as it would appear on the runway.

Flats: Include front and back flats for all garments, communicating the **construction** specifics of the products designed.

Illustrations: While some portfolio projects do not include **fashion illustrations**, they should be considered a valuable tool of creative storytelling.

Range board: Present each style in each color option in which it will be available. This board strengthens the communication of market awareness.

Lookbook/images of completed garments: This should be included if the garments themselves are not being shown during the delivery of the presentation. It is unnecessary to have both the physical garments and photos of them.

Spec packs: Including a handful of packs for key styles in the collection conveys the designer's strong grasp of production processes.

Including all of these elements in every project presentation ensures that the most important bases are covered.

Each designer is unique in their approach to the creative process. While focusing on personal brand value helps generate a consistent message for a body of work, designers must also consider the needs of their audience whenever presenting their portfolio. Early on in their training and career, designers are likely to present to a broad variety of groups, including press, recruiters, and buyers. Each audience type will expect to see certain specific items. Members of the press are more likely to be engaged by concept, creative process, original explorations, and artistic execution. Recruiters for design roles often want to see a balance of creativity and technical know-how, while recruiters for technical positions are likely to be fully focused on the latter. Buyers want to be shown how the line fits within the market and caters to the needs of their consumers, including a clear awareness of price point and production processes. The ability to edit the portfolio and customize it to particular viewers is therefore very important. When presenting to the press, for example, some of the spec-pack pages may be removed; if presenting for a technical design job, some of the more experimental process pages may be reduced.

While focusing each project toward one aspect or another is commonly done to make it more appealing to a given readership, portfolio projects should always appear complete. Each project should demonstrate a starting point, exploration, and conclusion that provide a sense

The review panel at ITS (International Talent Support) 2018. All young designers must become comfortable with presenting their work regularly to a broad variety of industry experts.

of perseverance and professionalism. Structuring a portfolio as a random collection of snapshots from a variety of projects should be avoided, as it is often confusing and unprofessional.

As a portfolio presentation is rarely longer than 15 minutes, the portfolio should be composed of about three or four fully developed projects. Trying to discuss all the work you have ever completed would be redundant and off-putting. The projects chosen for presentation should be decided according to your audience.

When starting out in the fashion industry, a young designer should determine a specialism that is driven by their creative interests and talents. This is important not only as a starting point for personal branding, but also to form the foundation of a designer's career path. The creative specialism chosen will determine which positions a designer will apply for, and in turn refine the possible audiences to whom a portfolio will be presented.

Effective Layout

Deciding how to lay out a portfolio presentation is a multifaceted challenge. Each page must be effective in its own right, work properly within the distinct project it belongs to, and contribute effectively to the entire portfolio. Multilevel planning is therefore required.

Page format and layouts

Start by considering the overall format of the portfolio being developed. Standard portfolio formats are usually no larger than 11 x 17 inches (28 x 43 cm), roughly A3 format, with all pages presented either in **portrait** or **landscape orientation**. Mixing page orientations should never happen as it makes the presentation awkward and messy. If working toward a portfolio book, designers should be aware that two pages will be seen side by side, making the full visual space of the portfolio **spread** double the size of the page chosen. This means that an 11 x 14 inch (28 x 36 cm) portrait page will produce a 22 x 14 inch (56 x 36 cm) spread, while an 11 x 17 inch (28 x 43 cm) landscape page will generate an 11 x 34 inch (28 x 86 cm) spread. Each page should be planned with this in mind.

Page layouts generally fall into two main categories: structured or organic. A structured page layout will place each element in clean alignments and organized arrangements to generate a tidy, effective, sometimes clinical result. Organic layouts, on the other hand explore collage techniques, either physically or digitally, to produce a creative, fluid, but at times potentially confusing page presentation. Regardless of the approach taken, the layout of each page should guide the eye of the viewer to a focus zone, likely to be the area that presents the largest image on the page.

Pages are usually structured according to simple grid layout guides (see opposite). Dividing each edge of the page evenly into 2, 3, 4, 5 or 6 units will produce a simple grid that can be used as a basic framework for planning the page. Whether implementing a structured or organic layout, following a grid can help to maintain some sense of overall organization and balance. Even with collage-like pages, there should be a sense of intentionality and care.

Storyboarding multipage presentations

Each multipage project presentation, as well as the overall portfolio, should be executed in such a way as to engage its viewer while also communicating the creative talents and technical abilities of the designer. The best way to ensure that a multipage presentation will work out effectively is to create a **storyboard** of it before launching into the execution of each page or board. Whether executed by hand or digitally, the storyboard will lay out a thumbnail of each spread in a proportionally correct manner so that the designer can visualize the entire project in one glance. This can be used to ensure that the layouts are dynamic enough to maintain the viewer's interest. The storyboard should determine how each spread will make use of scale, placement, **composition**, and graphic-design elements to make the overall presentation into an exciting visual experience. Repetitive or monotonous layouts can be identified at this stage, and should be replaced with more effective work.

PAGE LAYOUT OPTION WITH 3X3, 4X4, AND 5X5 GRIDS

3 x 3   4 x 4   5 x 5

A digital portfolio layout by Valeria Pulici.

Digital Portfolios

Designers greatly benefit from presenting their work online for the world to see. It enhances their public profile and increases their chances of recruitment, press attention, and creative collaborations. A personal portfolio website can offer great creative variety in how the work is presented, allowing designers to engage their audience through interactive content, multimedia communication, animated items, and much more.

Many recruiters today search out talent by browsing digital-portfolio platforms. These platforms include Behance.net, ArtsThread.com, Styleportfolios.com, Coroflot.com, and many others. Each platform differs in its navigational structure and searchability, as well as in its likely users. While some platforms are more popular with North American recruiters, others tend to be preferred by those based in Europe and elsewhere. Whatever the case, it is highly recommended that young creatives starting off in the industry showcase themselves on all the main portfolio platforms. While personal websites offer a more customized esthetic, the problem remains that these are very difficult to find unless someone already knows the designer's name or web address. Portfolio platforms therefore act as a valuable centralized venue, where recruiters can discover a designer's work simply by searching with a few key words.

Both personal-portfolio websites and portfolio-platform pages should always be linked to all of the designer's social-media profiles, such as Instagram, Facebook, Pinterest, Tumblr, and LinkedIn. Not doing so reduces the probability of their work being seen.

Each digital-portfolio platform organizes and presents visual material differently, which means that the portfolio work may need to be reformatted prior to publishing it so that it can best meet the visual structure of each platform. Behance organizes projects in a vertical page alignment, while ArtsThread pages are horizontal. Some platforms showcase only single-image items. The challenge for designers is

therefore to ensure that, regardless of the platform being used, the work is shown at its best. Developing platform-specific storyboards for the reformatting of work prior to publication is a valuable use of time.

A few simple technicalities, listed below, apply to all digital-portfolio platforms.

Page orientation: Most recruiters browse portfolio platforms on a computer screen, not a smartphone, which means that the work should be presented in a landscape page orientation. This can be achieved by employing a landscape page throughout all presentation work, reformatting work originally presented on portrait pages, or digitally combining two portrait pages together as a "spread" image before uploading it.

Resolution and image size: While images created for printing should be always be saved at a very high resolution (300 dpi/ppi or higher), uploading large files online can be challenging, and navigating them can be cumbersome for your intended viewer. For the purpose of digital publication, images should always be saved at a maximum size of 11 x 17 inches (28 x 43 cm), which is A3 format, and at 72 dpi resolution, flattening multilayered images to a single-layer copy.

Selecting a strong cover page: When recruiters browse through portfolio platforms, they often only get to see the cover page of most projects. The cover image is, in fact, what will make them decide whether to click on a project

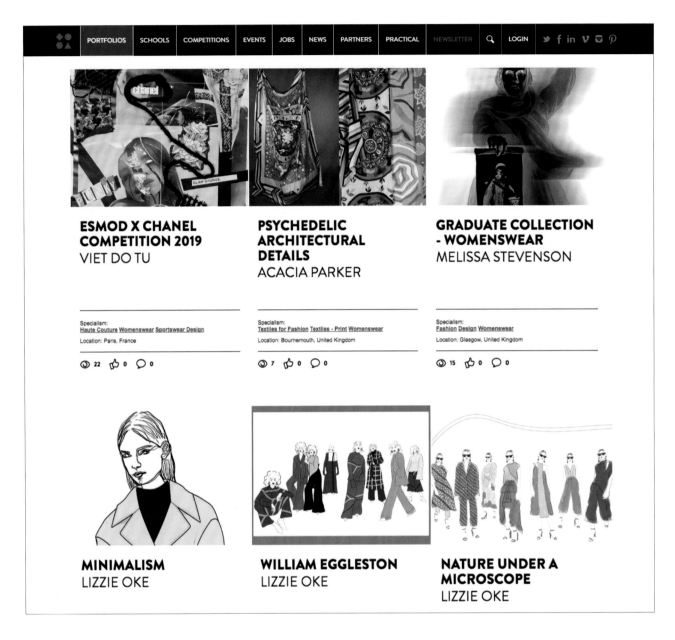

The cover image is the gateway to any digital portfolio, as shown on the ArtsThread site. Choose this image intentionally as is it very important to draw in your intended viewer.

and look at it in full. A strong cover page should engage the audience and display the creative talents and technical skills applied throughout the project.

Color management: When digitizing images, particularly when scanning or photographing hand-drawn illustrations or sketchbook pages, color balance often gets altered. The process of controlling color balance throughout all steps of visual communication is often referred to as color management. Digitizing two-dimensional work is best done using a scanner rather than photography, as scanners are usually calibrated for accuracy. On the other hand, documenting textiles, mock-ups, or garment samples can only be done with photography. In this case, the best way to ensure reasonable color accuracy is to document these items using diffused natural lighting. Regardless of the initial documentation process, every recorded image must be color-balanced, and images should then be viewed through a variety of devices to ensure the color management is consistent.

HORIZONTAL ALIGNMENT AND VERTICAL ALIGNMENT OPTIONS FOR DIGITAL PORTFOLIOS

HORIZONTAL ALIGNMENT

VERTICAL ALIGNMENT

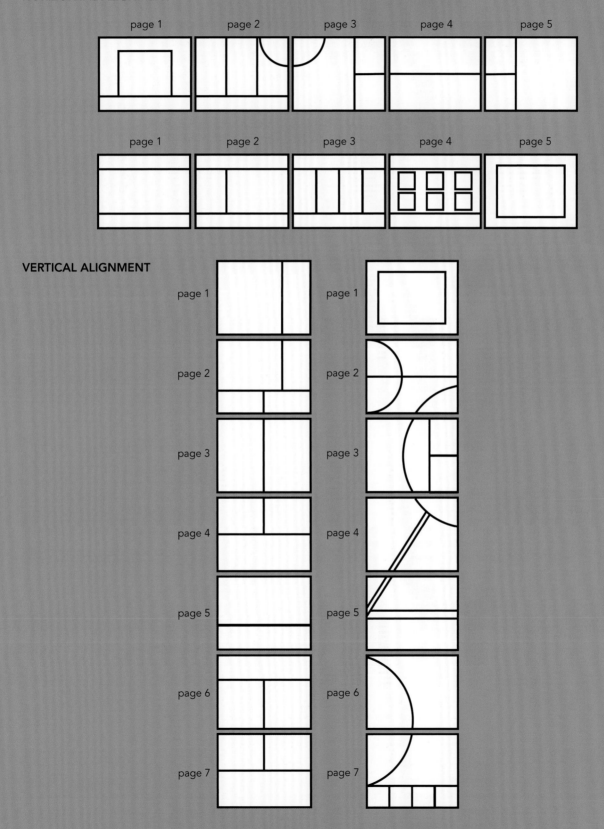

Résumés

The portfolio is the primary focus of most recruiters looking for design talent, but the value of a strong résumé should not be underestimated. Designers and creative professionals may at times find résumés dry and uninspiring, but these documents do provide quick and user-friendly information about applicants, which is essential when comparing one with another for the same position. While the primary purpose of résumés is to be clear and straightforward, designers often incorporate elements of personal branding into them. Personal logos may be added, or colors and fonts may be chosen to match the style of packaging used for the portfolio. These elements should be used with care so as not to detract from the clarity of the résumé.

Overall, the layout should be clean, easy to navigate, and clearly provide essential information. Personal details, such as name, address, phone number, and social-media handles, should be prominent, followed by a brief summary of core skills. When listing core skills, it is important to be truthful and informative. For example, listing "cut-and-sew apparel design" is much clearer than "**apparel**." While some designers like to include a brief personal statement of purpose, this often appears generic and tedious, in which case it should not be added.

Only educational and professional positions that have made a relevant contribution to career preparation should be listed. As such, while a college job in retail may be relevant for an entry-level application, it should probably be removed from the résumé later on in a designer's career. Overly complex visual material, such as large illustrations or overwhelming imagery, should be avoided. With that in mind, some designers may find they can successfully use simple graphic tools to convey their level of proficiency in professional software or their fluency in foreign languages. The entire résumé should be kept to no more than two pages, which can prove challenging.

Résumés should be concise, well organized, and easy to read.

BASIC RÉSUMÉ LAYOUT AND GRAPHIC-DESIGN ELEMENTS

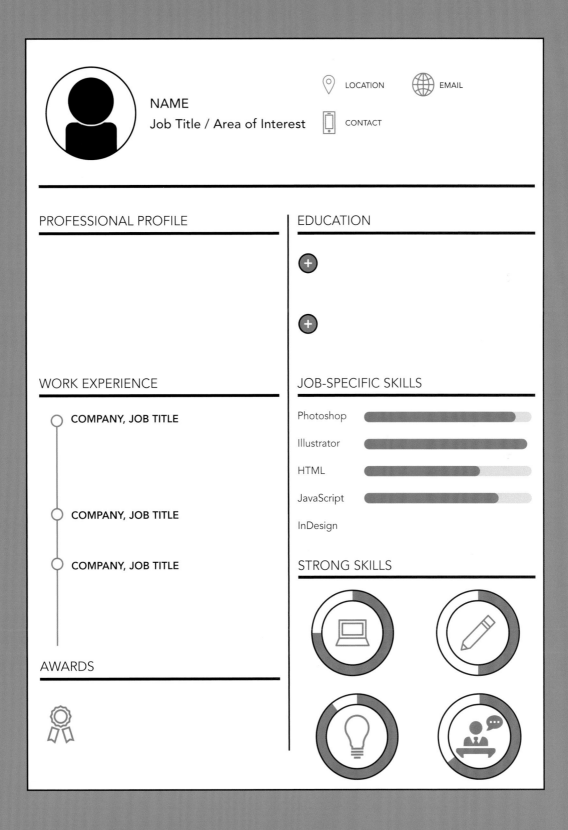

Essential Interview Skills

A professional interview can be nerve-racking, but remember, it is not an exam – it is an opportunity to connect with your audience and to tell them about yourself. When an applicant is asked for an interview, they should not forget that the recruiter has usually already seen their work in digital form, and believes the work itself shows the skills needed for the job. The only question remaining is whether the applicant will fit in with the team. While design training is often a very individually focused process, employment in the industry is always a team effort, so demonstrating the ability to gel within a team structure is paramount.

With this in mind, here are a few essential interview skills.

Research: Applicants should always research the company they are interviewing with, and make use of this information when preparing their talking points. They should focus on why they would be such a great fit for this company, based on how they can make a positive contribution to it. While pre-interview research should of course include collecting visual references of the company's work, it is also about acquiring a true appreciation of their approach to design and product. It is therefore important to include business news, relevant research into current trends, and any other information that might foster a deeper understanding of the brand and its context.

Listen, then talk with purpose: It is best to allow the recruiter to lead the conversation. Close attention should be paid when they speak, and responses should demonstrate that you have listened to them carefully.

Often young designers are afraid of silence, and feel the need to talk over it. The best way to avoid this mistake is to draw up a list of simple talking points for each project in the portfolio, having ensured they are organized in logical succession. When going over a project, the recruiter does not need to be told what can clearly be seen on the page. Instead, they will want to hear about the designer's unique creative approach, or the challenges encountered, and how these led to professional growth.

Self-confidence: In any interview it is important to make eye contact, avoid defensive body language, and think of the interviewers as friends. Workplaces thrive when teammates are motivated by real friendship toward one another, particularly in a field such as fashion design, where most aspects of daily activities and decision-making tend to be approached collectively. Design meetings, line-review meetings, marketing meetings, production meetings ... these are just a few of the many professional occasions that require strong interpersonal skills. Demonstrating a naturally friendly and open demeanor during the interview is therefore essential.

Opposite: A design presentation and interview at ITS (International Talent Support) 2018.

Recruiter Profile: Elaina Betts

Elaina Betts is a senior talent acquisition executive with JBCStyle Fashion Recruiters.

What made you want to become a fashion talent consultant?

I had no intention of pursuing fashion recruiting upon graduation. This career, like many wonderful things, came about organically and I am so grateful it did. At the core of every position I've held has been the principle of connecting the consumer to fashion through my work. Recruiting allowed me to unite my professional skill at connecting people and my personal passion for furthering opportunities for fashion creatives. Through recruiting, I've utilized my strong industry knowledge, personal experience in the market, fashion-specific education, and natural love of connecting others to aid creatives seeking professional development.

What skills do you feel are most important for young designers to showcase in their portfolio?

Design-process work, in my opinion, is the most important part of the candidate's portfolio. Our clientele are specifically interested in seeing both clean and esthetically pleasing hand- and fully **rendered croquis** sketching to judge the candidate's design ability.

Many young designers view the fashion industry as a cut-throat environment. Which personal aptitudes do you feel entry-level applicants should demonstrate?

Young designers should approach the industry with passion and persistence, and have an aptitude for retaining all knowledge given to them. This industry is competitive. However, it is not impenetrable for designers who seek it wholeheartedly, study their market of interest, network with other creatives, and take the time to absorb information as well as remain persistent in their pursuit!

What is the most important piece of advice you would give to young professionals entering the fashion industry?

I cannot stress enough how important it is for young designers to hone their personal esthetic and knowledge of their category of preference and market of interest, and then seek specific industry experience as soon as possible. Our clientele requests well-trained candidates with exposure in their individual market segment as well as category. Unfortunately, designers with extremely varied experience can read as a poor fit on paper. The "Jack of All Trades" can too often read as "A Master of None" with many potential employers. If a young designer's niche is Women's Advanced Contemporary, it is key that they train their eye, develop an aligned esthetic, and seek relevant experience in that market with established employers.

How do you foresee our industry evolving in the future? How do you think this will change portfolios, interviews, and other recruitment processes?

We are seeing a large increase of freelance, temp-to-perm and contract opportunities within the fashion industry and

Metropolitan Unique Bold Minimalist Contemporary

COLLECTION

Portfolio page by Manon Okel.

forecast that trend to continue. When permanent employment dominated market opportunities, short-term freelance experience could, unfortunately, handicap the candidate in regards to permanent hire. The change in market opportunities has shifted corporate stigma surrounding freelance employment and increased understanding of the benefits for all parties. There is also an increased personal preference for freelance work from candidates.

From the client standpoint, this freelance arrangement allows brands to test out a candidate's ability to mesh with their office culture, and review their performance capabilities and soft skills, prior to formal hiring. This also allows young designers to begin building relationships,

enhance their résumé, and receive corporate work exposure more quickly, while also continuing to seek permanent employment should they so choose. Additionally, the surplus of contract opportunities entices senior designers seeking to explore building their own labels: they can freelance and receive an income while building their brand, without the extra responsibility of a permanent position.

Glossary

Terminology can vary from country to country, so some terms listed in the glossary indicate the predominant usage first (usually from the U.S.A. or U.K.), and the next most common alternative in brackets. Creative teams outside of these regions tend to use the preferred terminology of their design managers.

Achromatic colors: White, black, and shades of gray, all of which contain no **hue**.

Analogous: A color scheme that uses **hues** directly adjacent to each other on the **color wheel** (e.g. blue + blue–purple + purple, or yellow + yellow–green + green).

Apparel (a.k.a. **Clothing**): Items of dress that cover the body, providing modesty and protection from the elements.

Appliqué: The technique of attaching decorative sections of fabric onto a base material. Appliqué is considered a subcategory of **embellishment**.

Beading: The decorative application of beads onto fabric, most often by sewing.

Belle époque: In French, "the beautiful period": the years 1871 to 1914, which saw the display of extravagantly ornate fashions in Europe.

Better (U.S.): A market level positioned between **bridge** and **moderate**. Brands such as Banana Republic and COS operate in the better market.

Bias: In a woven cloth, diagonal lines running at a 45-degree angle to the selvedges.

Bottom-weight fabrics: Materials suitable for the construction of trousers, but not tailored jackets. They include chino, denim, corduroy, and many others.

Brand identity: The cohesive message communicated by a company through its appearance, products, and services.

Bridge (U.S.): A market level positioned between **designer** and **better**. Brands such as Vivienne Westwood Red Label and Michael Kors operate in the bridge market.

Brushing: The process of altering the surface of a fabric by running it through a series of brush rollers. Brushed fabrics gain a soft touch (for example flannel) and, in some cases, a high sheen (such as brushed overcoatings).

Bubble-up trend (a.k.a. **Trickle-up trend**): A style originating from subcultural and street style, and imitated by higher-priced market segments.

Budget (U.S., a.k.a. **Mass-market**): The lowest-priced market level. Brands such a Faded Glory (Walmart), Old Navy, and Primark operate in the budget market.

Burnout (U.S., a.k.a. **Devoré**): A surface-decoration technique in which an acid chemical is applied to a mixed-fiber material such as velvet, satin, or jersey. The acid burns through some of the fibers but not others, creating an embossed or flocked surface appearance.

Cable knit: A technique used to add texture, usually with the appearance of braids or twists, to a **weft-knitted** fabric.

Category: A grouping of **apparel** defined by its functional purpose or production process. Woven tops, denim, **cut-and-sew knitwear**, and outerwear are all examples of apparel categories.

Classic: A style that gains popularity and retains it for a very long time. Denim jeans are an example of a classic style.

Collage: A creative methodology of **design experimentation** based on arranging separate items, such as fabric swatches and beads, extracted from research.

Color bar: A visualization of the colors for a clothing line or collection, balanced to reflect the proportional presence of each color involved.

Color management: The process of ensuring color consistency across multiple media and digital tools.

Color palette: The assortment of colors selected by a designer to be used in a clothing line or collection.

Color wheel: A visualization tool showing all hues in the color spectrum in a circle.

Competitive analysis: The process of researching and evaluating other companies that already operate in a given marketplace.

Complementary: A two-color scheme composed of **hues** found in diametric opposition on the **color wheel**, e.g. red–green or yellow–purple.

Composition: The arrangement of visual elements to create an object or image.

Concept: The creative direction or inspiration needed to guide the design-development process.

Concept board (a.k.a. **Inspiration board**): A visual summary of the creative concept used to lead a design process or collection.

Conceptual design: A creative approach focused on developing new approaches to the design and production process.

Construction: The way in which garment pieces are assembled into a finished item of clothing.

Consumer segmentation: The dividing of consumers into smaller groups.

Consumption: The purchasing of goods and services that are incorporated into daily life.

Contractor: A business paid to produce garments, textiles, trims, or other components on behalf of **manufacturers** and according to their specifications.

Control measurements: Reference measurements provided to a **contractor** to ensure that the garments they make meet required sizing standards.

Costing: The tabulation and prediction of production costs for a designed item prior to its being produced and sold.

Costume: A style of dress belonging to a cultural group, social class, profession, or national identity. The term "costume" is also used in discussions of historical style.

Course: A horizontal row of stitches in a **weft knit**.

Crewelwork: A type of embroidery, generally executed with wool thread, popular in Great Britain in the 1600s.

Croquis (a.k.a. **Fashion sketch**): A quick visualization of an outfit on an elongated standing or walking human form. *See also* **rendered croquis**.

Cross grain: In a woven cloth, this is the direction of the threads running at a 90-degree angle to the selvedge.

Crushing: A surface manipulation requiring the heat-setting of somewhat random creases in a fabric. Crushing velvet not only generates these creases, but also randomly flattens the pile, giving the fabric a "shattered" look.

Customer profile: A visualization of a customer's lifestyle and esthetic preferences.

Cut-and-sew knitwear: A garment category based on cutting and assembling pieces of knitted fabrics, such as jersey, fleece, and velour.

Dart: In garment construction, a V-shaped tuck that is added to provide dimensionality and volume to certain areas, such as the chest, back, shoulder, or hip.

Deconstruction: The process of taking garments apart, or constructing garments in ways that look intentionally unfinished or raw.

Demographics: A consumer-research process based on quantifiable data such as age, sex, geographic location, education, or employment.

Designer (market level): The highest-priced **ready-to-wear** level of the fashion industry. Designer-level brands regularly showcase their products through runway presentations.

Design experimentation: The second phase of the design process, which focuses on creatively exploring all the possible design applications of the **concept** and research.

Design imitator: A company or brand that copies existing styles and trends in order to maximize profits.

Design innovator: An individual, company, or brand that generates innovative, forward-thinking products, unrestricted by current commercial trends.

Design interpreter: A company or brand that creates product incorporating both marketplace awareness and moderate creative innovation.

Design methodology: An approach to the creative process. Examples include **croquis** sketching, **collage**, draping, and 3D modeling.

Design refinement: The final stage of design processing, focused on styling, editing, and finalizing the range or line in 2D.

Diffusion line: A line of **apparel**, or other fashion-related products, developed by a **manufacturer** and sold at a cheaper price point than their chief brand.

Digital draping: A variety of digital approaches to design visualization.

Digital printing: A printing technique that employs computerized machinery to apply a digital image directly onto fabric.

Dip-dyeing (a.k.a. **Ombré**): The partial application of dye to yarn or fabric; a technique used mainly to achieve a gradient of color.

Double complementary: A four-color scheme composed of two sets of complementary colors.

Double knit: A technique of simultaneously knitting two threads, usually of different colors, into a thicker, multicolored final fabric.

Dress: The collective term for all the items and practices used by a population to protect and adorn the human body. Among these are clothing, jewelry, makeup, and footwear.

Dress form (a.k.a. **Form** or **Stand**): A three-dimensional replica of a human body, used instead of a live model during draping and garment development.

Editing: The process of preparing a body of work for public presentation by correcting, condensing, or otherwise modifying it.

Editorial: Photography or writing expressing the viewpoint of an editor. Editorial photography is usually styled and shot in order to achieve advanced esthetic values.

Embellishments: A family of decorative techniques used to beautify fabric. **Embroidery, beading, appliqué**, and **sequin** work are all forms of embellishment.

Embossing: A process in which a raised stamp is pushed into a material to alter the surface.

Embroidery: The decorative use of sewing techniques to **embellish** the surface of a fabric.

Engineered (surfaces): Printed or **embellished** designs planned with the three-dimensional form of the garment in mind so that the resulting visual pattern flows elegantly across **seams** and **darts**.

Fabric trade show: A professional gathering of individuals and companies operating in the textile industry. Most fabric trade shows are set up in such a way that all participating textile producers can showcase their products and services to **apparel manufacturers**.

Fabrication: The making of cloth by manipulating fibers or yarns. Felting, weaving, and knitting are types of fabrication process. Solution-based fabrication, achieved by solidifying plastics, is used to produce materials such as vinyl and polyurethane. The term "**fabrications**" is commonly used to refer generically to fashion materials.

Fad: A trend that gains very rapid and intense popularity, then fades away just as quickly. It is most likely to attract teenage consumers.

Fair Isle: A type of knitting characterized by repeating multicolored geometric patterns. This technique generates horizontal strands of yarn, called floats, on the reverse side.

Fashion: A style that gains temporary popularity and widespread use at its peak, only to be replaced by a different style shortly thereafter. The term can refer to modes of dress, music, food, or any other consumer product. It is also commonly used as synonym for the most popular style of dress.

Fashioned knitwear: A garment category produced by knitting yarn into shaped **apparel** pieces, and then linking these to form finished garments.

Fashion illustration: An artistic, **editorial** visualization of a fashion look.

Fiber: The smallest component that makes up textile materials. Fibers can come from natural sources (e.g. silk, cotton, wool, or linen), or be manufactured (e.g. rayon, polyester, nylon).

Filament fibers: Fibers harvested or produced as single long continuous strands, such as silk and rayon.

Findings: An umbrella term for all the elements, other than outer fabrics and decorative trims, that are needed to construct a garment. Findings include shoulder pads, interfacings, canvas interlinings, and closures.

Finishing: The process applied to fabrics to complete their production and make them market-ready. Finishings can be esthetic, such as printing and **embossing**, or functional, such as fireproofing and boiling.

Flat drawing (a.k.a. **Flats**)**:** A proportionally accurate drawing of a garment, using line-drawing techniques and intended to communicate the exact proportions and construction details of the item. Usually executed in black line on a white background.

Form: *See* **Dress form**.

Garment fitting: The process of using 3D draping methodologies to refine the shape and proportions of existing garments with a view to including them in a design line.

Gatekeepers: Important decision-makers within the fashion industry, for example influential editors in the fashion press, trend forecasters, and buyers and merchandisers for major retailers.

Gauge: The number of stitches per 1 inch (2.5 cm) in a horizontal row of knitting. The number varies according to the size of yarn, the size of needle, and the stitch. The number is commonly used to indicate the weight of knitted materials, 30 gauge being very fine and 7 gauge being very heavy.

Generational cohort: A consumer segment focused on the shared behavior of people born within a certain time period (generation).

Geometric pattern experimentation: The process of draping geometrically cut areas of fabric on the **dress form**.

Grain: Usually refers to the direction of lengthwise threads in a woven cloth. These run parallel to the **selvedge**, the most stable direction.

Graphic print: A type of print pattern in which the design is visibly separated into a small number of distinct colors.

Greige goods: Unfinished textile materials, which can be dyed, printed, or otherwise finished to the requirements of the manufacturer to address consumer demand. **Muslin** (calico) is a greige good used in producing garment samples and **mock-ups**.

Haute couture: A market level focused on the production of custom-designed and custom-made **apparel** that is created and produced exclusively for one client. It often involves extensive use of hand-construction methods. *Haute couture* is French and translates as "high sewing."

High street (U.K. – a.k.a. **Mall** in U.S.)**:** A market segment focused on wide accessibility. Brands found in the main shopping streets of the United Kingdom can all be considered high-street brands, somewhat regardless of price level.

Hue: A specific mix of primary colors, such as cyan (pure primary), purple (secondary), or yellow–orange (tertiary). Any hue can then be used as the starting point for further color development, by adding white or black to create either a **tint** or a **shade** of the base hue.

Ideation: The process of developing ideas, research directions, and design possibilities from an initial **concept**.

Innovator: *See* **Design innovator**.

Inspiration board: *See* **Concept board**.

Intarsia: A technique used in knitwear to produce multicolored single-layer fabrics.

Interpreter: *See* **Design interpreter**.

Jacquard: A mechanized weaving technique that produces complex woven patterns, able to achieve intricate multicolored designs in the fabric.

Jersey: A plain knitting fabrication that alternates purl and knit stitches so that each is visible on one or other side of the finished cloth.

Landscape orientation: *See* **Page orientation**.

Laser-cutting: The process of etching or cutting through fabric with the use of a computer-controlled laser.

Layout: In a visual presentation, the way in which text and pictures are set out on a page.

Lifestyle inspiration: A type of **concept** focused on the needs, wishes, habits, or aspirations of the consumer.

Lineup: The visualization of a collection of outfits as a series of **croquis** sketches or **rendered croquis** placed side by side.

Logo: A symbol or image used by a brand to identify its products and services.

Lookbook: A printed or digital publication created for displaying styled images of completed sample garments.

Macrotrend (a.k.a. **Megatrend**): A long-term trend expressed in widespread changes in consumer behavior over five or more years.

Manufacturer: A business that creates new product and sells it to **retailers**. In this case the product sold is referred to as **wholesale** merchandise.

Market level (a.k.a. **Market segment**): A subcategory of the fashion industry, most commonly defined by the price of the items being manufactured and sold.

Market opening: An area of the marketplace not currently served by existing companies.

Mass-market (U.S.): *See* **Budget**.

Merchandising: The activity of enhancing sales of a brand. This commonly includes promotions and visual presentation of the brand and its products. The merchandising team is often responsible for advising the design team about which products should be included or excluded from a line.

Middle Ages: A period in Western history spanning from the end of the Roman Empire (c.400 CE) to the beginning of the Renaissance (c.1400 CE).

Mind mapping: A technique used to record ideas generated by brainstorming. It takes a central starting point and organizes ideas along linear and cluster arrangements.

Mock-up (a.k.a. **Sample prototype**): A test production of a garment detail, or part of a garment, in **muslin** (calico) or other cheap fabric for the purpose of working out its technical requirements and assessing its design viability.

Moderate (U.S.): A market level positioned between **better** and **budget**. Brands such as Gap and Zara operate within the moderate market level.

Modular design: A design methodology that combines styles and details from a predetermined library of usable elements.

Monochromatic: A color scheme composed of only one **hue**. This may still include the use of **tints** and **shades**, or the inclusion of **achromatic colors**.

Monopolistic competition: A competitive strategy that seeks to convey a sense of uniqueness about a company's products or services.

Mood board: A visual representation of the emotional communication embodied in a designed collection of **apparel**.

Mordant: A chemical mixed with dye to enhance its effect on fibers or other material. Using a mordant makes the resulting dyed material more vibrant and less prone to fading.

Moulage: From French for "molding," the process of draping fabric on a **form** to achieve a self-supporting garment shape and establish the volume and construction of a garment.

Muse: An inspirational person, commonly used by designers to enhance their creative process. Muses often embody the designer's ideal consumer.

Muslin (fabric) (U.S. – a.k.a. **calico** in U.K.)**:** A **greige good**, usually woven in unbleached cotton and used in the development of garment samples and **mock-ups**. Muslin is produced in a variety of weights, from light shirting to heavy canvas. When developing a muslin mock-up, designers should select the weight that best reflects the properties of their chosen final fabric.

Muslin prototype (U.S. – a.k.a. **Toile**)**:** A garment sample or working prototype executed in muslin fabric (calico) or other cheap material.

Narrative theme: A type of **concept** focused on storytelling. Narrative themes often take creative inspiration from places, environments, time periods, or particular cultures.

Niche: A narrowly focused area of the marketplace.

Ombré: *See* **Dip-dyeing**.

Packaging: The presentation of a brand or product through the use of wrapping or protective materials.

Page orientation: The format of a page or image. Those with the longer edge horizontal are said to be in **landscape** orientation, while those with the longer edge vertical are in **portrait** orientation.

Patchwork: A surface-manipulation technique requiring multiple segments of fabric to be sewn together to create a larger area of cloth.

Perforation: A tiny hole. Perforations are commonly made in fabric by using die-cutting machinery.

Photographic print: A type of print pattern that uses the full spectrum of color.

Placement print: A type of print design that appears in a distinct area of a garment. Slogan T-shirts are examples of placement prints.

Pleating: A surface manipulation requiring the heat-setting of permanent controlled creases in a fabric.

Portfolio: An edited presentation of a designer's body of work.

Portrait orientation: *See* **Page orientation**.

Postmodernism: A philosophical and artistic movement that developed in the mid-20th century. Postmodernism is associated with the ideas of self-referentialism, relativism, pluralism, and irreverence.

Primary colors: Blue, red, and yellow. These colors can be mixed in various combinations to form all the other **hues** on the **color wheel**.

Primary research: Information gathered first-hand – through direct observation, drawing, photography, videography, surveys, interviews, questionnaires, or focus groups.

Process book (a.k.a. **Sketchbook**)**:** A book, folder, box, or digital file in which research investigation, **design experimentation**, and **design refinement** processes are documented.

Product developer: A professional within the fashion industry who manages the execution of **apparel** items from approved design to finished product.

Production run: The product quantity required for distribution to **retailers**.

Psychographics: A consumer-research process based on gathering qualitative information such as preferences, values, and tastes.

Purl knitting: A knitted fabric that uses only one type of stitch (purl), generating a material that looks the same on both sides.

Quilting: The technique of sewing two or more layers together to form a thick, padded material. Quilting can be done by hand or machine and generates a textured effect on the material.

Range board: A visualization of a complete line grouped into garment categories, and including all colorway options for every garment.

Ready-to-wear (a.k.a. **RTW** and **Prêt-à-porter**): Any **apparel** produced in standard sizes.

Rendered croquis: A fully executed **croquis** sketch, using advanced visual-rendering techniques and media, to accurately communicate the surfaces present in the look. Rendered croquis are used primarily in presentation **lineups**. They are sometimes wrongly referred to as **fashion illustrations**.

Repeat print (a.k.a. **Allover print**): A type of print design that appears to cover the entire surface of a garment seamlessly.

Research investigation: The first phase of the design process, which focuses on extracting inspirational creative elements from the raw research.

Resist-dyeing: A process in which wax or a chemical are applied to fabric to prevent it from absorbing dye in certain areas. *See also* **Wax-dyeing.**

Resolution: The number of pixels or dots per inch in a digital image. High-resolution images (a minimum of 300 ppi/dpi) are required to ensure suitable print quality, while screen-resolution images (72 dpi/ppi) are better for digital publication.

Résumé: A brief summary of qualifications, education, and professional history, which is used for job applications. It is sometimes known as a **Curriculum Vitae** or **CV**.

Retailer: A business that sells product to the final consumers or users.

Ruching (a.k.a. **Gathering** or **Shirring**): A surface-manipulation technique in which fabric is crumpled or scrunched together through the use of elastic or basting (tacking) stitches.

Sample yardage (a.k.a. **Sample cut**): A length of fabric ordered by an **apparel** manufacturer from a textile mill for the exclusive purpose of producing the prototype garments, also referred to as runway or sales samples.

Sandblasting: An abrasive surface treatment applied to fabric and finished garments, in which an air compressor fires sand over the material to make it look worn or aged.

Saturation: The visual intensity or vibrancy of a **hue**.

Screen printing (a.k.a. **Silk-screening**): A printing technique in which images are applied to fabrics or underlying layers through a stencil that is held in place by a fine mesh or screen.

Seam: In garment construction, the area where two garment pieces are joined together, usually by sewing.

Seasonal color (a.k.a. **Fashion color**): A color used within a clothing line for a short period of time.

Seasonal fabrication: A fabric or material used in a design line for only one season. Such materials convey the creative innovativeness of the seasonal collection.

Secondary colors: The **hues** achieved by mixing two **primary colors** together (e.g. green comes from combining blue and yellow).

Secondary research: Information gathered from existing sources, such as books, magazines, and journals.

Selvedge: The finished edge of a woven cloth, running along the lengthwise edges of a cut of fabric.

Separates: A range-planning approach that focuses on creating a variety of interchangeable garments instead of complete outfits, in order to give the consumer greater styling choices.

Sequin: A flat, shiny disc used to ornament clothing. Some sequins can be pressed into faceted cup shapes for added shine. The word "sequin" derives from the Italian *zecchino*, a type of metal coin.

Serging machine (a.k.a. **Serger** or **Overlocker**): A family of machines used in **apparel** production for finishing the cut edges of garment pieces, or for the assembly of **cut-and-sew knit** garments.

Shade: A color derived from mixing any **hue** with black.

Shibori: A family of **tie-dyeing** techniques that originated in Japan.

Showpiece: An outfit designed to create visual impact in a runway presentation. Showpieces strengthen the brand narrative and can attract press attention, but are often too complex to be suitable for commercial production and distribution.

Silhouette: The overall shape of an outfit.

Smocking: A surface-manipulation technique in which folded fabric is stitched together to create a textured surface. Smocking is often associated with rustic or ethnic dress styles and children's apparel.

Specification/Spec drawing: A line drawing, sometimes considered to be a subcategory of **flat drawing**. Specification drawings are proportionally accurate visualizations of garments, and include close-up views of details, internal construction, etc.

Specification/Spec pack (a.k.a **Technical/Tech pack**): A multi-page document aimed at communicating all the necessary information regarding a style for the purposes of production.

Split complementary: A three-color scheme formed of a **hue** from one side of the **color wheel**, and two hues sitting next to its direct **complementary**.

Spread: In a book, two pages facing each other.

Staple color: A color used repeatedly within a clothing line over a period of time. Neutrals and **achromatic colors** are commonly employed as staple colors.

Staple fabrication: A fabric or material that appears repeatedly within a clothing line over multiple collections and over a long period of time. These materials are likely to generate regular, consistent sales.

Staple fibers: Fibers that occur naturally or are produced in short segments, such as wool and cotton.

Stonewashing: A finishing process, commonly used in denim manufacturing, in which cloth or garments are washed with stones to impart an aged look.

Storyboarding: The process of visualizing multipage presentations by using thumbnail images to establish the placement of content and layout elements.

Style code (a.k.a. **Style name**): A code used to identify each style to allow for easy tracking during sales, production, distribution, and retail.

Styling: The process of collating style elements, including garments, accessories, hairstyles, and makeup, to create a cohesive brand message and reveal the story behind a line presentation or **editorial** photoshoot.

Supply chain: All the steps or processes involved in the production and distribution of a product.

Surface draping: The process of draping fabric on the **dress form** to add a textured surface to a supporting undergarment.

Editorial illustration
by Nataša Kekanović.

Tambour: A frame used for holding large fabric pieces in place during **embroidery**. Tambour embroidery is used extensively in *haute couture*, and requires a specialized hook rather than regular sewing needles.

Taste: An esthetic preference. Taste can be individual, or shared by a social or cultural group.

Technical/Tech pack: *See* **Specification pack**.

Technical drawing: A line drawing that shows a detail or functional aspect of a garment.

Tertiary colors: The **hues** achieved by mixing a **primary color** with a **secondary color** (e.g. blue–green, or red–purple).

3D printing (a.k.a. **Rapid prototyping**): The computerized process by which a digital 3D model can be produced as a physical three-dimensional object.

Tie-dyeing: A process in which a fabric is tied or placed under pressure to prevent certain areas from absorbing dye.

Tint: A color derived by mixing any **hue** with white. Such colors are sometimes referred to as pastels.

Tolerance: The allowable amount of discrepancy between the measurements of an approved sample garment and the measurements of that same style assembled during a **production run**.

Trapunto: A subcategory of **quilting**, this uses larger amounts of padding, fiberfill, or cords to achieve a thicker raised surface.

Trend: A change in **taste** or esthetic preference over a period of time.

Trend forecasting: The process of predicting the future movement of trends through research and analysis.

Triadic: A three-color scheme composed of colors evenly spaced on the **color wheel**, e.g. red + blue + yellow, or yellow–orange + red–purple + blue–green.

Trickle-across trend: Style trends that originate anywhere within the marketplace and gain instant and widespread popularity through mass-communication and agile **supply-chain** management.

Trickle-down trend: Style trends originating from high-end **innovators** and fashion leaders, and imitated by lower market segments.

Trim: An element used decoratively in the construction of a garment, such as ribbons, **appliqués**, and closures (when used as **embellishments**).

Tucking (a.k.a. **Pintucking**): A surface-manipulation technique in which folds are sewn to create a rippled effect.

Typography: The style and appearance of letters and words in digital or printed matter.

Vat-dyeing: A process in which yarns or fabrics are dyed by holding them in a basin or pot of dye, generally referred to as a vat.

Vertical integration: A strategy used to maximize profits by taking direct control of multiple stages within the supply, manufacturing, production, distribution, and retail chain.

Vintage: A category of historical clothing, usually less than 100 years old, which has maintained or regained stylistic appeal.

Visualization: The process of bringing an idea into 2D or 3D form.

Wale: The vertical alignment of stitches in a **weft knit**.

Warp: The threads lying parallel to the **selvedge** in a woven fabric.

Warp knit: Knitted fabric in which the yarns predominantly move in the lengthwise direction of the cloth.

Wax-dyeing: A subcategory of **resist-dyeing** that uses only wax (rather than chemicals) to prevent certain areas of fabric from taking the dye.

Weft: The threads lying perpendicular to the **selvedge** in a woven fabric.

Weft knits: Knitted fabrics in which the yarns predominantly move in the widthwise direction of the cloth.

Wholesale: Selling items to **retailers** who then sell them on to consumers. Generally, wholesale pricing is between a third and a half of the retail price.

Woodblock printing: A technique in which images are applied to fabric by using carved stamping tools.

Yarn: A thread usually resulting from spinning (or twisting) **fibers** together. The finest filament yarns made of synthetic materials may be produced of a single unspun fiber.

Yarn-dyed fabrics: Woven or knitted materials constructed from yarns that have been dyed before fabrication occurs. Solids, **jacquards**, and striped and checked materials are commonly constructed as yarn-dyed fabrics for improved durability of the color.

Zeitgeist: A German term meaning "the spirit of the times." In fashion, the decorative arts, and other cultural expressions, it refers to the esthetic pervading a particular region and period.

Fashion materials

and their

common uses

Fabrics and materials in the fashion industry are commonly categorized in standard groupings, which helps designers to determine how each material should be applied to specific garment categories. Following these guidelines can ensure that a designer's product aligns with all of the other product already on the marketplace.

Use-based Groupings

Fabrics are often referred to by their predominant use, but designers can nonetheless use them in other garment categories if they wish.

Shirtings: Intended for use in woven (button-up) shirts and blouses. Shirtings may be further subdivided in lightweight, midweight, and heavyweight groupings, which offer further guidance as to their likely seasonal use.

Bottom-weight fabrics: Intended for use in trousers, shorts, and skirts. Bottom-weight fabrics may at times also be usable for making casual jackets.

Suitings: Fabrics used for suits (jacket and trousers or skirts). Suitings are further categorized in weight groupings, ranging from the lightest tropical weights (ideal for warm summer days) to heavyweight suitings (best used for winter tailoring). Midweight suitings are intended to be worn year-round in a business environment.

Jacketings: Intended for the construction of blazers, jackets, or sports coats. Jacketings are usually too heavy to be used for tailored pants.

Coatings: Intended for use in outerwear garments, such as raincoats and blousons.

Overcoatings: Considered by many to be a subcategory of coatings, overcoatings are usually intended exclusively for tailored topcoats and overcoats.

A look from the 16N Fall 2019 collection, making use of a variety of fabric weights.

Weight-based Groupings

In an effort to standardize the process of categorizing fabrics, many manufacturers refer to materials not by their suggested use (as listed on page 197) but instead by the weight of the fabric. Weight is measured either in ounces per square yard (oz/yd^2), or in grams per square meter (gsm or g/m^2). This system relates to the physical properties of cloth rather than its presumed purpose, so can feel less limiting for designers.

Fabric-weight conversion chart

g/m²	oz/yd²	g/m²	oz/yd²	g/m²	oz/yd²
50	1.47	220	6.49	390	11.50
60	1.77	230	6.78	400	11.79
70	2.06	240	7.08	410	12.09
80	2.36	250	7.37	420	12.38
90	2.65	260	7.67	430	12.68
100	2.95	270	7.96	440	12.97
110	3.24	280	8.25	450	13.27
120	3.54	290	8.55	460	13.56
130	3.83	300	8.84	470	13.86
140	4.13	310	9.14	480	14.15
150	4.42	320	9.43	500	14.74
160	4.72	330	9.73	510	15.04
170	5.01	340	10.02	520	15.33
180	5.31	350	10.32	530	15.63
190	5.60	360	10.61	540	15.92
200	5.90	370	10.91	550	16.21
210	6.19	380	11.20	560	16.51

To convert a gsm measurement to ounces, multiply the number by 0.02948.
To convert an ounce measurement to gsm, multiply the number by 33.92.

Opposite: A weaving loom in a textile factory.

Croquis and

flat templates

Womenswear croquis templates

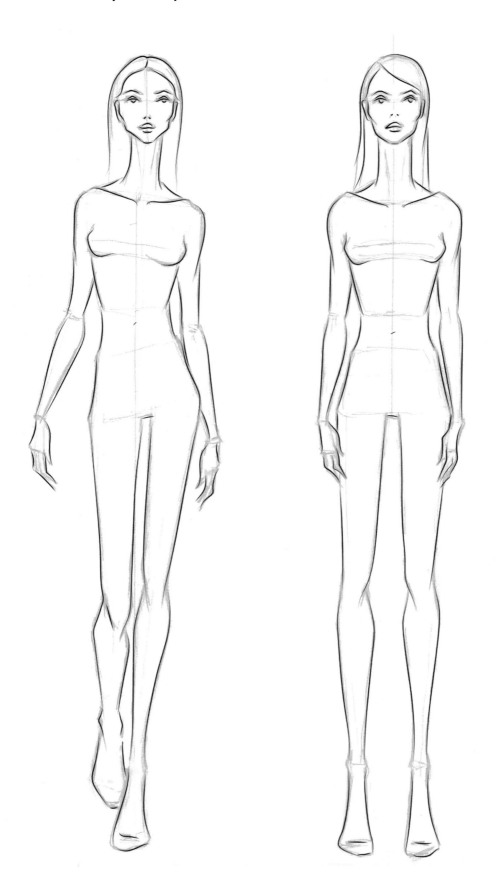

Menswear croquis templates

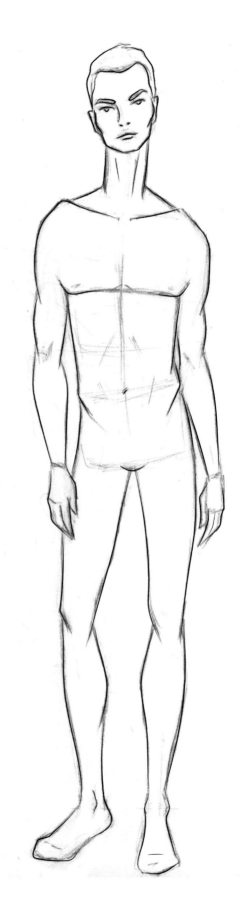

Maternity and plus-size croquis templates

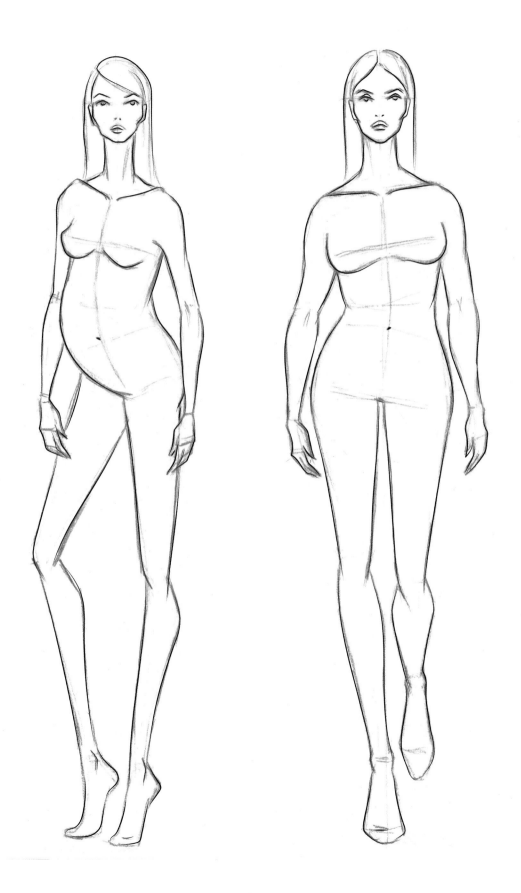

Childrenswear croquis templates

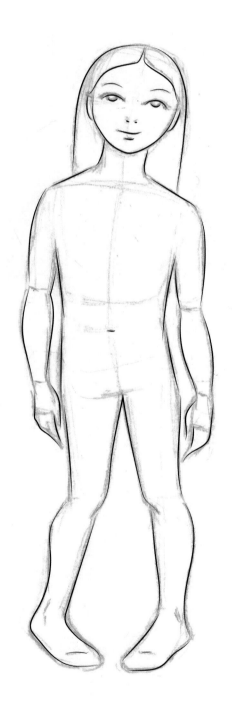

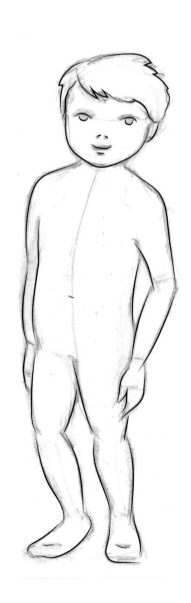

Flat templates

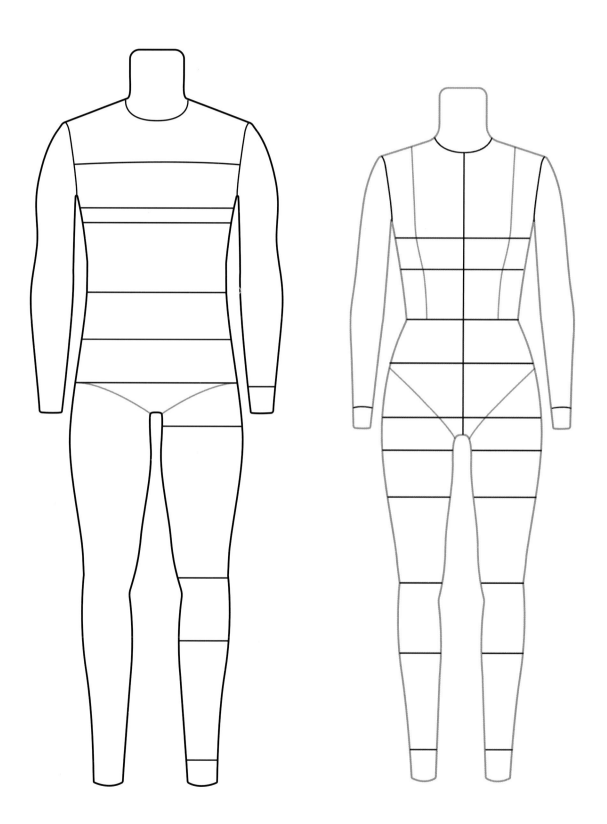

Flat reference library

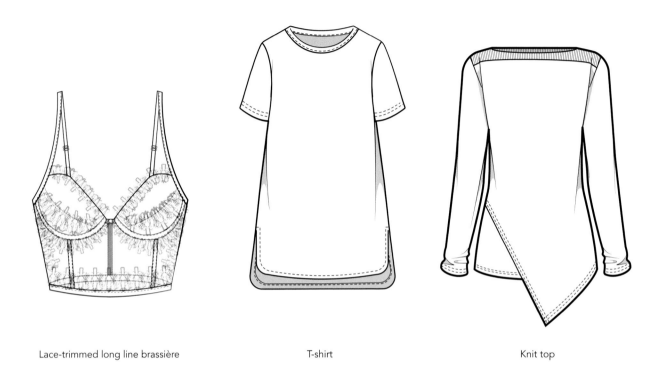

Lace-trimmed long line brassière

T-shirt

Knit top

Zip-front leggings

Kimono

Beaded swimsuit

Oversized boyfriend shirt

Handkerchief-hem skirt

Balloon skirt

High-waisted slacks

Dungarees

Western jeans

Two-layered slip dress

Ruched cocktail dress

Peasant dress

Safari dress

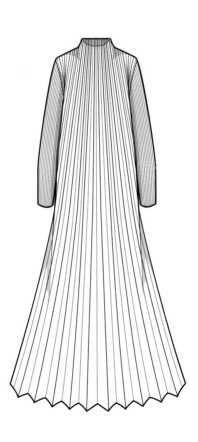

Pleated maxi dress

Mermaid dress with
organza capelet

Textural cable-knit sweater

Boxy Fair Isle pullover

Cowl neck cut-and-sew knit top

Moto jacket with
decorative patches

Layered perforated
leather bomber

Puffer coat

Fur-trimmed coat

T-shirt

Polo shirt

Classic button-up shirt

Utility shirt

Piped detail resort shirt

Swim trunks

Boxy tailored shorts

Hoodie

Cardigan

V-neck cable-knit sweater

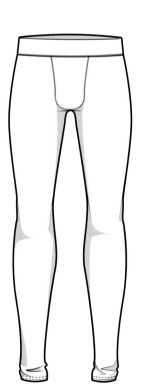

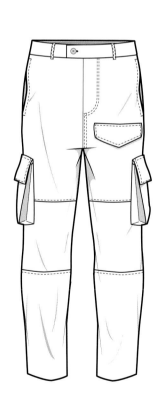

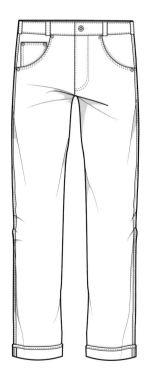

Men's leggings

Sweatpants

Cargo pants

5-pocket selvedge jeans

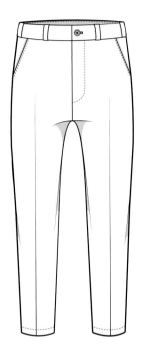

Tapered slacks

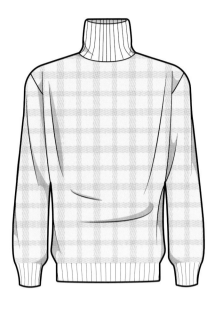

Intarsia turtleneck sweater

Utility vest

Pinstripe double-breasted jacket

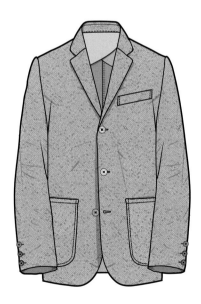

Half-lined deconstructed tweed jacket

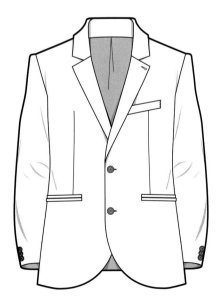

Slim-fit two-button single-breasted jacket

Bomber jacket

Denim jacket

Corduroy worker jacket

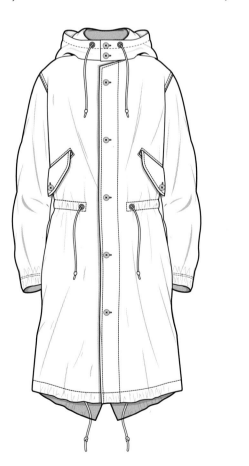

Parka

Double-breasted Chesterfield

Useful

resources

Fashion and Costume Research

Museums

Balenciaga Museum – Getaria, Spain
Bata Shoe Museum – Toronto, Canada
Christian Dior Museum and Garden – Granville, France
Fashion Museum – Bath, U.K.
FIDM (Fashion Institute of Design & Merchandising)
  Museum and Galleries – Los Angeles, California, U.S.A.
Fondation Pierre Bergé–Yves Saint Laurent – Paris, France
Gucci Museum – Florence, Italy
Kent State University Museum – Kent, Ohio, U.S.A.
Kobe Fashion Museum – Kobe, Japan
Kyoto Costume Institute – Kyoto, Japan
Les Arts Décoratifs – Paris, France
Metropolitan Museum of Art (Costume Institute) –
  New York City, New York, U.S.A.
ModeMuseum (MoMu) – Antwerp, Belgium
Museo de la Moda – Santiago, Chile
Museo Frida Kahlo – Mexico City, Mexico
Museo Salvatore Ferragamo – Florence, Italy
Museum at FIT (Fashion Institute of Technology) –
  New York City, New York, U.S.A.
Museum of Bags and Purses (Tassenmuseum Hendrikje) –
  Amsterdam, The Netherlands
Museum of Fine Arts and Lace (Musée des Beaux-Arts
  et de la Dentelle) – Alençon, France
Palais Galliera – Paris, France
Palazzo Fortuny – Venice, Italy
SCAD FASH (Savannah College of Art and Design
  Museum of Fashion) – Atlanta, Georgia, U.S.A.
Simone Handbag Museum – Seoul, South Korea
Victoria and Albert Museum – London, U.K.

Magazines

This list includes fashion periodicals both current and discontinued, all of which can be valuable sources of fashion research.

7th Man – U.K.
10 Men – U.K.
Allure – U.S.A.
An an – Japan
AneCan – Japan
Another – U.K.
Another Man – U.K.
Arena Homme + – U.K.
Asian Woman – U.K.
Burda Style – Germany
Café – Sweden
CanCam – Japan
Classy – Japan
Cliché – U.S.A.
Complex – U.S.A.
Cosmode – Japan
Cosmopolitan – U.S.A.
Crash – France
Darling – U.S.A.
Dazed & Confused – U.K.
Details – U.S.A.
Egg – Japan
Elle – France and India
Esquire – U.S.A.
Fantastic Man – Netherlands
Fashion – Canada
Fashion Central – Pakistan
Fashion Forward – Israel
Femina – Denmark, Indonesia, and India
FHM India – India
Flaunt – U.S.A.
FRUiTS – Japan
Fucsia – Colombia
Fujin Gaho – Japan
GQ – U.S.A.
Grazia – Italy and India
Grind – Japan
Happie Nuts – Japan
Harper's Bazaar – U.S.A.
i-D – U.K.
InStyle – U.K. and U.S.A.
JJ – Japan

Koakuma Ageha – Japan
L'Officiel – France
L'Officiel Hommes – France
L'Uomo Vogue – Italy
Look – U.K.
Lucire – New Zealand
Lucky – U.S.A.
LTST – U.K.
Marie Claire – France
Men's Non-no – Japan
Men's Vogue – U.S.A.
Modelatude – India
Model Bank – Dubai
nicola – Japan
No Tofu – U.S.A.
Non-no – Japan
Numéro – France
Numéro Homme – France
Nylon – U.S.A.
Nylon Guys – U.S.A.
Olivia – Finland
Oyster – Australia
PAPER – U.S.A.
Pinky – Japan
Pop – U.K.
Popeye – Japan
PopSister – Japan
Popteen – Japan
Purple – France
Ranzuki – Japan
Schön! Magazine – U.K.
Seventeen – Japan and U.S.A.
Sneaker Freaker – Australia
So-en – Japan
Teen Vogue – U.S.A.
V – U.S.A.
VMAN – U.S.A.
Verve – India
Vestoj – France
Vivi – Japan
Vogue – China, France, India, Italy, U.K., and U.S.A.
Vogue Hommes International – France
Vogue Knitting – U.S.A.
W – U.S.A.

Trends and Consumer Behavior

Trend forecasting

www.edelkoort.com
www.fashionsnoops.com
www.f-trend.com
www.trendcouncil.com
www.trendstop.com
www.wgsn.com

Consumer and market research

The Business Research Company
Euromonitor International
Global Industry Analysts
GlobalInfoResearch
IMARC Services Pvt. Ltd.
LP Information Inc.
MarketLine
QYResearch Group
TechNavio – Infiniti Research Ltd.
Textiles Intelligence

Academic Journals

Clothing and Textile Research Journal
Costume: The Journal of the Costume Society
Critical Studies in Men's Fashion
Fashion Practice: The Journal of Design, Creative Process & the Fashion Industry
Fashion, Style and Popular Culture
Fashion Theory: The Journal of Dress, Body & Culture
Film, Fashion and Consumption
International Journal of Fashion Studies
Luxury: History, Culture, Consumption
Textile History

Further Reading

Africa Rising: Fashion, Design and Lifestyle from Africa by Robert Klanten et al. (Gestalten, Berlin, 2016)

CAD for Fashion Design and Merchandising by Stacy S. Smith (Fairchild Books, New York, 2012)

The Chronology of Fashion: From Empire Dress to Ethical Design by N.J. Stevenson (A&C Black, London, 2011)

Creative Fashion Design with Illustrator® by Kevin Tallon (Batsford, London, 2013)

Design Your Fashion Portfolio by Steven Faerm (Bloomsbury, London, 2011)

Drawing Fashion: A Century of Fashion Illustration by Joelle Chariau, Colin McDowell, and Holly Brubach (Prestel Verlag, Munich, 2010)

Fashion Design by Elizabeth Bye (Berg, Oxford, 2010)

Fashion Design by Sue J. Jones (Laurence King Publishing, London, 2011)

Fashion Design Course by Steven Faerm (Barron's, Hauppauge, NY, 2010)

Fashion Design: The Complete Guide by John Hopkins (AVA Publishing SA, Lausanne, 2012)

Fashion Design Research by Ezinma Mbonu (Laurence King Publishing, London, 2014)

Fashion Drawing Course: From Human Figure to Fashion Illustration by Juan Baeza (Promopress, Barcelona, 2014)

Fashion Drawing: Illustration Techniques for Fashion Designers by Michele W. Bryant (Laurence King Publishing, London, 2016)

Fashion: A History from the 18th to the 20th Century: The Collection of the Kyoto Costume Institute by Akiko Fukai et al. (Taschen Bibliotheca Universalis, Köln, 2015)

Fashion Illustration & Design: Methods & Techniques for Achieving Professional Results by Manuela Brambatti and Lisa K. Taruschio (Promopress, Barcelona, 2017)

Fashion Illustration by Fashion Designers by Laird Borrelli (Chronicle Books, San Francisco, 2008)

Fashion Thinking by Fiona Dieffenbacher (AVA Publishing, London, 2013)

Fashion: A Visual History from Regency & Romance to Retro & Revolution by N.J. Stevenson (St Martin's Griffin, New York, 2012)

The Fine Art of Fashion Illustration by Julian Robinson and Gracie Calvey (Frances Lincoln, London, 2015)

The Fundamentals of Fashion Design by Richard Sorger and Jenny Udale (Bloomsbury Visual Arts, New York, 2017)

Groundbreaking Fashion: 100 Iconic Moments by Jane Rocca and Juliet Sulejmani (Smith Street Books, Melbourne, 2017)

Knit: Innovations in Fashion, Art, Design by Sam Elliott (Laurence King Publishing, London, 2015)

Pattern Magic by Tomoko Nakamichi (Laurence King Publishing, London, 2010)

Pattern Magic 2 by Tomoko Nakamichi (Laurence King Publishing, London, 2011)

Pattern Magic 3 by Tomoko Nakamichi (Laurence King Publishing, London, 2016)

Pattern Magic: Stretch Fabrics by Tomoko Nakamichi (Laurence King Publishing, London, 2012)

Patternmaking by Dennic C. Lo (Laurence King Publishing, London, 2011)

Patternmaking for Fashion Design by Helen J. Armstrong (Pearson, London and New Delhi, 2014)

Patternmaking for Menswear Gareth Kershaw (Laurence King Publishing, London, 2013)

Print in Fashion: Design and Development in Fashion Textiles by Marnie Fogg (Batsford, London, 2006)

Sewing for Fashion Designers by Anette Fischer (Laurence King Publishing, London, 2015)

Textile Futures: Fashion, Design and Technology by Bradley Quinn (Berg, New York and Oxford, 2010)

Zero Waste Fashion Design by Timo Rissanen and Holly McQuillan (Fairchild Books/Bloomsbury Publishing, London, 2016)

Index

Picture credits

Acknowledgments

Lyons, Leeds College of Art, 2015; 128r Davide Maestri/ WWD/Shutterstock; 130l Daniel Vedelago; 130r Denis Antoine; 131 Courtesy Hold.com; 132 Pixelformula/Sipa/ Shutterstock; 133 Courtesy Aitor Throup Studio, aitorthroup.com; 134 Caryn Lee; 135 Amanda Henman; 136 Jousianne Propp; 137 Denis Antoine; 138 Marina Meliksetova/Mélique Street; 139 Eva Boryer; 140a @Steve Benisty; @Whitewall.art; 140b, 141l & r @ CucculelliShaheen; 142 Gabriel Villena; 143 Jousianne Propp; 145 Denis Antoine; 146l Shutterstock; 146r Amy Sussman/WWD/Shutterstock; 147 Siting Liu; 148 Gabriel Villena; 150l Ashley Whitaker; 151 Nataša Kekanović. Commissioned by SHOWStudio for Milan Fashion Week Menswear A/W 2017; 152l Gabriel Villena; 152r Alina Grinpauka; 155l & r Jousianne Propp; 159 VecFashion/ Templatesforfashion.com; 161 Nikki Kaia Lee; 162 Courtesy Christopher Raeburn; 164 Constance Blackaller; 165 Courtesy ITS. Photo Pablo Chiereghin/ITS 2018; 167 Paola M. Riós; 168 Portfolio by Momoko Hashigami, courtesy ITS, photo Daniele Braida/ITS Creative Archive; 169a Courtesy Joseph Veazey/JosephVeazey.com; 169b Kevin S. Warwick. Private Collection; 171 Courtesy ITS. Photo Giuliano Koren/ITS 2018; 174 Valeria Pulici; 178 Pixel-shot/Shutterstock; 181 Courtesy ITS. Photo Daniele Braida/ITS 2018; 182 Elaina Betts; 183 Manon Okel; 193 Nataša Kekanović; 197 Imaginechina/Shutterstock; 199 Alba_alioth/Shutterstock.

Illustrations for Laurence King Publishing by Johnathan Hayden 28, 78, 79b, 87l & r, 91, 105, 125, 129, 149, 154, 156–157, 173, 177, 179, 205–213; and Lara Wolf 150r, 201–204.

The author wishes to extend his thanks to all who have contributed to this title: Helen Ronan, Sophie Wise, Clare Double, and Giulia Hetherington at Laurence King Publishing and those who provided valuable guidance throughout the peer-review process, as well as all contributors of visual material shown throughout, with a special mention to Lara Wolf and Johnathan Hayden for their work.

The author also wishes to thank his husband Paul Emmons, and his daughters Daphne and Penelope for their unending patience and support throughout this endeavor.

Finally, special thanks go to all those who teach fashion. Every single day, teachers contribute positively to the growth of individual students, and shape the future of the entire fashion industry. The professors I was guided by during my studies, and the colleagues I have had the pleasure to work with to date, all greatly deepened my appreciation for the meaning and value of what fashion teachers do every day. This book is therefore dedicated to them.